Fred Brown moved fro
several years ago and n
East Kent.

By the same author

Happy: The Life of a Working Sheepdog
The Grass is Greener

FRED BROWN

Badgers in our Village

GRAFTON BOOKS

A Division of the Collins Publishing Group

LONDON GLASGOW
TORONTO SYDNEY AUCKLAND

Grafton Books
A Division of the Collins Publishing Group
8 Grafton Street, London W1X 3LA

A Grafton Paperback Original 1990

A CIP catalogue record for this book
is available from the British Library

ISBN 0-586-20517-9

Printed and bound in Great Britain by
Collins, Glasgow

Set in Janson

Acknowledgement
The author and publishers are grateful to Ernest Neal and Croom
Helm for permission to reproduce a passage from *The Natural
History of Badgers* by Ernest Neal (Croom Helm, 1986).

To celebrate Jason and Tamsyn

Author's Note

For a quarter of a century I lived and worked in London, loving every moment, never dreaming of moving away, least of all deep into the country. But now, a decade or so after such a move, this book continues the story begun in *The Grass is Greener*, with particular reference to badgers.

As before, I have sometimes changed the chronology and treated two or three similar personalities and events as one, never, however, going outside the essential nature and spirit of my own experience.

Special thanks to Alan Mustoe, skilled in a dozen rural crafts, whose friendship in six months taught me more than my own flounderings in the previous six years; to Martin Newcombe, for so readily sharing with me his vast working experience of badgers; and most of all to Muriel, without whom I, never mind the book, would hardly have taken this shape.

Contents

1

Badgers in the nick

There is a sort of badger-watchers' grapevine. All outsiders are treated with suspicion, for our anxiety is not to pass on information, directly or indirectly, to the wrong types. Badger-baiters do exist!

So I wasn't a bit surprised to learn in a typical round-about way that one of the biggest setts in the country was in the grounds of a prison. My informant regretted he couldn't speak with the authority of what he himself had seen, but rumour, speculation had it . . . The trouble is, he concluded, there's no admission for non-offenders; the only way to get in is to break the law.

I consulted with other badger-watching addicts. They smiled knowingly and shrugged their shoulders. You won't, they confirmed, get in otherwise.

It seemed crazy, yet it made sense. No security-conscious staff could tolerate visitors poking around reputedly looking for badgers. The possibilities for less innocent goings-on would be endless, a nightmare for those responsible for keeping residents *in*, never mind undesirables *out*. Even so, the thought of all those badgers remaining unwatched! Tantalizing. Finally unbearable.

I pressed the bell at the main gate. A spy hatch was opened. Then a narrow door, wide enough to admit one person at a time, revealed a friendly face. I was still kept standing on the outside.

'The badgers,' I said. 'I hear you have badgers in here.'

'Badgers!' His mouth fell open.

'That's right,' I said. 'Badgers. You know, *badgers*.'

His smile no longer involved his eyes; with practised scrutiny he looked me up and down.

'Badgers, you say?'

'I wondered,' I said, 'whether you could let me in, just to have a look.'

He paused, briefly lost for words, perhaps mentally flipping through the rule book.

'You'll have to write to the governor,' he said. 'That's a matter for him.'

'I only want,' I explained, 'to see the sett, then perhaps come back to watch – one night about an hour before dusk!'

'Now listen,' he jollied me along, 'it's beyond my authority. Only the governor could grant permission for something like that. You'd better write to him. All right?'

And the door, like the spyhole, was firmly closed. I was still on the outside.

I went home, wrote my letter, and waited. But not for long, even less than return of post.

Can you imagine picking up the phone, and hearing 'Hello, this is the governor speaking'? Unnerving, I can tell you. Especially – and here, I realize, I'm revealing more about myself than the governor – especially as he sounded so incredibly human. My unquestioned assumption was that he, no less than his staff, would of necessity be tough, an unyielding stickler for discipline, devoted to the letter of the law, resolute in dotting every 'i' and crossing every 't' of regulations. Yet here he was, the governor himself, assuring me he'd be simply delighted to put his badger inmates at my disposal. Absolutely delighted.

'It's good to know someone's so interested,' he said.

Nor was he finished. The sett or setts, he explained, were some distance from the main gate. Would it help if he arranged transport?

'Could I also bring my dog?' I asked.

'Dog!' His voice gave a first hint of caution. 'I should have thought a dog and badgers wouldn't mix.'

'Only when I look at the sett or setts,' I explained, 'not when I actually watch for the badgers. She's beautifully behaved; won't cause any trouble. But if you'd rather I didn't . . .'

'No, no,' he said. 'I don't mind at all. You know your own business. I would, though, appreciate a brief report of anything you find. We're all interested and protective of the badgers, you see, anxious they shouldn't be disturbed. Our problem is time. You could help us to keep an eye on things, if you follow.'

I did.

What a charming man.

The very next afternoon I presented myself at the main gate.

'Ah, the badger man,' said the smiling bunch of keys. 'Transport should be here in a few minutes.'

I climbed in.

'Ah, the badger man,' said the driver.

We drove to a checkpoint adjacent to woodland.

'Ah, the badger man,' said the officer behind the counter. On hand was an assistant governor who chatted about his lovely working environment as he escorted me past another checkpoint, guided me to the woods and pointed to where he thought the badgers were in residence.

All the cast-iron surveillance as I was passed on from one prison officer to another was accompanied, I must say, by remarkable courtesy, and a practical helpfulness far beyond either my deserts or needs. Without exception these men appeared massively interested in the badgers. They said they liked them around the place, wanted to know as much about them as possible, and welcomed me as a likely informant. My dog and I were free – relatively speaking, you understand – to roam the woods to our hearts' content.

And within minutes I was staring with incredulity at a concentration of dung pits such as I'd never seen before. I should explain, badgers – unlike foxes and most other wild creatures – relieve themselves with discrimination; not in any old place but into pits they themselves dig for the purpose. The number I found almost immediately suggested this was some sett! And the further I searched, dung pits aplenty confirmed that here was a sizeable social group extending to most parts of the woods.

Clearly visible runs or paths were everywhere, for badgers are essentially creatures of habit, using the same routes as they leave and return. This explains why I had no difficulty finding one cluster of entrances after another, some of them exceptionally big in diameter, with signs of recent digging by the badgers; loose earth piled high on already massive mounds. Nearby these clusters were large areas virtually free of all vegetation but trees, where the bracken had been pushed back and the undergrowth on the peripheries flattened – evidently play areas for the badgers before their main business of looking for food.

Confidently I chose my spot for watching, halfway up an ideally positioned tree, and planned to return after forty-eight hours; enough time for my scent and the dog's to be blown away.

As things turned out, my return was delayed for a further twenty-four hours by a tropical-like downpour.

The officer at the first checkpoint welcomed me back like an old friend; the officer at the second, just as friendly, lamented that the night before last a badger had been killed on a nearby public road, doubtless an accident. We shared commiserations that thousands were slaughtered in like fashion every year, and wondered what, if anything, could be done about it.

Then I disappeared into the woods, watched by this prison sentinel who regretted his lack of freedom to join me – a remark of unconscious irony, I thought, in the circumstances.

As usual, I had arrived an hour and a half before dusk, confident this would give me plenty of time to climb my tree and settle before the badgers bestirred themselves. Casually, thinking more of the lovely surroundings than the badgers, I approached. Two were waiting to greet me! I had no cover, I simply stood gazing at them as they appeared to be gazing at me, or at least in my direction. They made no attempt to scarper or acknowledge my presence, but merely larked about with each other, chasing, shuffling on their backsides, mutually grooming, before disappearing up an incline, presumably towards a source of food.

I didn't hang about. I went up that tree with the alacrity of a man twice my age, anxious to be well out of sight when the prima donnas still below put in an appearance. Almost immediately two obliged, coming from my left and darting into an entrance. One of them – I supposed it was one of the same two – reappeared and made off in the direction of the earlier couple.

For perhaps ten minutes nothing further happened – nothing further, that is, apart from a cow bulling in the distance, a crow cawing like mad and being answered in like cacophony, and rabbits chasing each other among the trees, totally oblivious of my nearby perch.

Unfortunately the same could not be said of all life in the vicinity. Possibly you too have known the feeling – behind you, always behind you, a pair of eyes are watching; boring into your back; finally making it impossible not to turn round or at least glance over a shoulder. Slowly I looked behind me – and found myself staring into a face professionally qualified to be suspicious on or off duty. In no other way could this prison officer have picked me out of my hide. I was camouflaged, wrapped in leaves of a beautiful hazel. It made no difference.

Gotcher!

His look of triumph penetrated my very soul.

I stayed up the tree. He advanced a couple of feet, still unbelieving. Puzzled. Determined. I panicked. If he came any nearer, made the slightest noise, my badger-watching for the night was finished almost before it started. Yet manifestly he had no intention of going away, not before apprehending me, positively not before I'd explained myself.

I put my index finger across my mouth, silently shushed, and mimed a solitary word:

Badgers!

His face registered both alarm and incomprehension.

Once more my desperate silence shouted:

Badgers!

And I turned my back or rather my head to concentrate on the essential purpose of my unexplained presence.

Only later, as I reported at my first checkpoint, did I learn of the sequel. Still suspicious, baffled why a bearded stranger with a funny hat – a sure sign of decadence – should be halfway up a tree within the confines, he nipped to the nearest checkpoint, fortunately my second, to make enquiries. His colleagues roared with laughter, and one of them immediately decided it was time for him personally to share my badger vigil. Happily he wasn't so successful at spotting me, a fact we mourned together at the appropriate time!

16

Of course, while all this was going on unknown to me, I was still up the tree; waiting, hoping the prison officer's devotion to duty hadn't disturbed the badgers. I didn't need to hope for long. Within five minutes of his departure, a veritable procession commenced.

One, two, three, four, five badgers, nose to tail, a sow and four cubs, emerged from an entrance no more than twelve strides from my perch. Magic. And such is the illogicality of badger-watchers, I found myself actually regretting the prison officer's disappearance and wanting if possible to attract his attention to this black and white ballet.

Have you ever seen badger cubs at play?

No?

You haven't lived.

Ask any badger-watching addict. Cubs at play are a celebration of life. Entertainment. Fun. Wonderful. These four wrestled, rolled over and under each other, grunted, squealed, snapped. Two of them 'fought' the sow; another ran halfway up the incline before scarpering back as though being chased; one chased its own tail. Finally all four laid into the sow, jumping on her as she gently pushed them off her prostrate body, allowing them at times to trample all over her, making no attempt to curb such playful pestilence.

Then she was on her feet, leading them up the incline for the serious business of feeding. Incidentally, seeing she herself was capable of devouring over a hundred earthworms before dawn, you can imagine that every single one of that species in the wider area faced a somewhat precarious night!

The next three badgers to emerge, one a magnificent boar, didn't hang about within my vision. True, they engaged in a bit of mutual sniffing and grooming, the boar shuffled on his bottom, appeared to clip one of the sows behind the ear and proceeded to rough up both of them a little before the happy trio wandered off up the same incline, the route for all the badgers I'd seen so far.

Dusk was now beginning to close in. For perhaps twenty minutes nothing further happened. Time to withdraw, I decided. It was, however, still quite light, too early to give up hope of more sightings. Why not, I thought, stroll back to my checkpoint via the dung pits; a slight detour with no danger of losing my way. I felt profoundly satisfied, light-hearted, already more than rewarded, and almost indifferent whether I saw additional badgers or not. Stealth hardly marked my approach.

Yet there, twenty strides in front of me, was a sow with three cubs. I froze. The quartet continued their antics, never still for a moment, dancing, rolling over and over in wrestling embrace, snarling, biting (painfully, judging by the squeaks and squeals), totally unaware of my presence. And when, fifteen minutes or so later, I withdrew, no longer able satisfactorily to see, they were all presumably too preoccupied having fun to care whether I stayed or went.

It was the very first watch on which *I* had left the badgers rather than the other way round.

The prison officer who'd failed to find me wanted a full report when I checked in – or more accurately *out* – at security. And unhurriedly, like a couple of successful conspirators, we swapped experiences, he as much enchanted by these lovely creatures as I.

What a prison.

What inmates.

I'm hoping for a long sentence!

2

The case of the missing badger sett

Badgers!

It's hard for me to believe now that not so long ago I barely realized they existed. Theoretically, of course, I knew they did – creatures of the night, shy, venturing stealthily, hypersensitive to danger, especially their only real predator: man. Not being a countryman, it never seriously crossed my mind that I might actually see one. And even long after we moved to the country, this same assumption prevailed. Their world was secretive, safely tucked away from prying eyes.

A good job too!

Furthermore, quite a number of villagers born and bred hereabouts, some longer ago than they care to acknowledge, aren't ashamed to confess they've never seen a badger.

Foxes? Legions of 'em. But badgers! They are altogether a different proposition, much less numerous, well off the beaten track, their setts hard to find, the badgers themselves harder still to see.

I hear this comment, almost lament, times without number. On second thoughts, not so much lament as resignation. Badgers are like dormice and kingfishers – known about but never seen; or rarely seen, and then only by experts who know precisely where and when to look.

A farmer near our cottage told me there used to be a sett on his land, years ago. He pointed in the general direction.

'Saw a fox in that region recently,' he said. 'Bloody foxes! I'd skin 'em all alive if I had my way.'

He also told me, not batting an eyelid, of a particular fox during what he called his 'annual culling' of foxes on his own and neighbouring farms.

Having picked it out by raking a field with the beam of his torch, its eyes shining like diamonds, he'd attracted it towards himself and his partner by sucking on the back of his hand to make a squeaking or squealing noise like a rabbit in distress. The fox had come on apace, attracted irresistibly by the prospect of an easy feed. Getting nearer, it had stood momentarily, obviously bewildered by this audible yet invisible prey, and then started to circle the imagined quarry. Round and round. Time after time.

Intrigued, both men had simply watched this (for them) unique behaviour, one still sucking, the other forgetful of his gun. Then almost reluctantly he'd taken aim, fired, and blown off one of the fox's legs.

Still it had continued to circle, held captive by the squeaking and squealing, seemingly indifferent to the missing leg. Another shot, this time bang on target.

In case you might be wondering, I should in fairness mention that both men are caring of all animals, farm stock and wild alike; caring but not sentimental – and sick at heart that a second shot had untypically been necessary. But they remain unrepentant about the annual culling, insisting that without it their farms and those nearby would be overrun with foxes.

I wonder.

But, then, I don't own a sheep farm, with newborn lambs frequently taken, as they claimed, by foxes. If I did, and the evidence of such killings confirmed the foxes' guilt, I should no doubt share their attitude. As it is, I continue to enjoy every sighting of these wily creatures, my affection and admiration reinforced each time.

I suppose I feel about foxes as the farmer claims to feel

about badgers. I say *claims* because, even as he told me, I couldn't help but detect a note of reservation. Well, judge for yourself. He said he had found a lamb with its head bitten off and its throat torn. Definitely the work of badgers, he assured me.

Now admittedly badgers eat lambs as carrion, but virtually never stalk and pounce on them. In any case, why, I asked, would a badger kill a lamb and then leave it? For the sheer hell of it, the pleasure of the kill!

Definitely a badger, he repeated; no question, no question at all. He knew the signs of a badger when he saw them!

On one thing, however, we were agreed. The badger, if such it was, didn't live on his farm or anywhere else we knew, or even suspected, near our village. It must have been on a foray from a distant sett. We didn't have any badgers in our village!

So you can imagine my astonishment when – on my way to the woods on what passes for our main road – I saw my very first badger.

Dead.

Apparently killed by a car or lorry, and lifted to the grass verge. I gaped in unbelief. True, I knew that thousands were slaughtered in this way every year, but actually to come across one – I repeat, my very first – stopped me in my tracks. And we didn't, as you know, have badgers in our village.

This apart, the sight of such a lovely creature lifeless overwhelmed me for a moment or two. I stood there riveted to the spot, trying to take in the evidence of my own eyes; and racing through my mind was a deduction surely not unworthy of a Sherlock Holmes: somewhere in the vicinity there must be a sett. Simply had to be.

* * *

I asked around. No, we didn't have badgers. Not now. Definitely. Not for years; somebody must have dumped the one I saw. But by now I didn't doubt this badger had lived nearby, within a mile at most, I calculated – though why a mile I have no idea. For all I knew, badgers travelled much longer distances. At the time, my ignorance settled for a mile.

I searched. A waste of time. I didn't know *what* I was looking for, and I didn't really know *where* either. But I persisted, and eventually – as I've told elsewhere* – I found a sett, tucked away in a part of a wood rarely visited, with the ruins of a long-deserted cottage lost in the under-growth, a sett no more than a fifteen-minute walk from our cottage. Naturally I mentioned this to no one, at first, anxious the badgers should come to no harm. I can't think of anyone in our village who would harm a fly, let alone a badger, but once people start talking, undesirable outsiders' ears might be listening.

One thing led to another. I often watched at the sett – *my* sett, as I like to think of it – captivated by badgers at play, inwardly chuckling at some of their antics, charmed most of all by cubs on the rampage; but all the time that dead badger wouldn't lie down. Did it really come from this sett? I wasn't sure. For a start, I found another sett, admittedly slightly further away, but still, I thought, feasible, well within the magic mile I'd fortuitously picked out of nowhere. And supposing there were other setts, nearer the point of my killed badger? The notion appealed because by now I was beginning to realize that, even in our badgerless village, these lovely creatures of the night were about, possibly in number. I had the satisfaction of hugging to myself a secret unknown even to the veteran villagers.

* *The Grass is Greener* (Grafton, 1988)

Perverse, I admit, but that's how it was – the smugness of the ex-townee among seasoned countrymen!

All this was shortly before a villager whose hens had been taken by a fox pointed out to me what she suspected was the culprit's earth. Not that either of us, you appreciate, meant the fox any harm, reasoning that you can't blame a fox for being a fox; but as we picked over the bones and feathers, doubtless from her hens, the thought crossed my mind that all these entrances were too many for an earth, surely. Could it be that badgers were also about?

The main entrance to the earth, littered with pieces of numerous prey, was self-evident. But the more I looked at the other entrances the greater became my excitement. For their shape was different, not the vertical oval characteristic of an earth, but a horizontal oval, sign of a badger's work. The close proximity didn't bother me. I knew that foxes and badgers were known sometimes to share not remotely the same home, but certainly part of the same underground complex; another mystery to me, for how come a clean badger tolerates the nearness of an animal notorious for its dirty habits?

None the less, all doubt was cast aside when I found a dung pit! Remember? A fox – like some dogs on our village green – defecates in any old place; a badger digs a hole before relieving itself into it. Once full, it digs another and another, usually on the boundary of the sett, well out of the way. This dung pit was full. *Full.*

Hang on a moment! It was also, on closer inspection, too old for an occupied sett. If badgers *were* about, they hadn't shit in these parts for some time. This must be an outlying sett, a sort of standby for emergencies – disturbance at the main sett, for instance, or to be used as a birth chamber during the cubbing season. And it was no more than a small field away from where I had come across the dead badger. There had to be link, if not directly, at least with the main sett. We'd discovered a lead, thanks to a marauding fox.

So where to look now? The obvious place from where we were standing was a private wood on the far side of a grain field, no more than three hundred strides or so away. Fortunately the owner, a farmer, had a reputation for being a conservation enthusiast; a glance at the land he'd recently flooded as a haven for wildfowl and the like suggested the possible happy combination of successful farming and concern for the environment. Not all farmers are vandals – not even most! This one, however, was among the very best. I know. The first time we talked together he confessed his love for foxes. The second time, like a conspirator sharing a secret he would guard with his life, he told me about the heronry in his wood, to which more and more pairs were returning after a lapse of some years.

Confidently I knocked on his door.

I told him of our discovery of what we believed was an outlying sett, and my wish to search in his wood for a possible main sett. 'Badgers!' he exclaimed, and recollected setting a snare for a fox raiding the henhouse and taking lambs – years ago – and catching a badger. Despite his antagonism to the fox, he'd set the snare with reluctance, driven to it, not sure what else to do. Finding the badger had added to his wretchedness.

His only concern was to release it. *Its* only concern was to remove his fingers, if not hand, as he tried. Finally, he threw a sack over its head, stood astride a pole on its neck and cut the wire; not, he added, without difficulty!

The badger, now free, stayed where it was. Just sat. Made no attempt to scarper.

He tried to chase it away. It didn't budge. Simply sat staring at him as though the wire still held it. Three times that day he went back, and still the badger was there, resistant to his shooing and waving of arms. Next morning it was gone.

'Wonderful creatures, badgers!' he said.

I asked him about the heronry and told him I'd been watching it through binoculars from the grain field. His face beamed. He oozed with pride and pleasure.

'I think it's firmly re-established,' he said; 'a few more pairs this year.'

The way back to our discussion of badgers was circuitous! Probably he was weighing me up, making up his mind whether or not I could be trusted. But, finally convinced, he confessed to the existence of a sett in his wood, pointed out the relevant area and assured me I was welcome to search and watch – the proviso being, of course, that I mentioned nothing to anybody else. Proof of his love for badgers!

Within six or seven minutes of leaving his farmhouse I was in the wood, across a plank bridging a babbling stream, and staring with growing excitement at entrances, runs, play areas, dung pits – all the signs of badger occupation, plus another telltale indicator. Flies were hovering in some of the entrances, caught in a catch-22 situation – attracted by the smell of the badgers but too repelled by the darkness to seek them out. An old countryman once told me that, having found a new sett, this was the first thing he looked for, infallible evidence of the badgers being in residence.

All that remained was for me to return next day at dusk, or perhaps the day after, to watch.

My wife told *me* to calm down. Would I, she fussed, be all right in the woods in the dark on my own? Did I have a torch? What if I lost my way or had an accident?

I sauntered round the grain field, focused my binoculars briefly on the heronry, noticed what looked like a rook colony not all that far away, checked the direction of the breeze and crossed the plank. There was at least an hour before twilight. Rabbits scurried, one lingering at the mouth of an entrance, seemingly undecided about whether to venture in. I knew that badgers and rabbits coexisted quite happily, that each sometimes took over the abandoned burrows of the other; but normally they ignored each other, though the badger, snuffling out a nest of baby rabbits, ate the lot. In my ignorance I did wonder what would happen if a badger emerged from the entrance at which the rabbit was preening itself.

Slowly the gathering darkness transformed distant trees into sinister shapes, quickening my imagination, emphasizing my total aloneness – humanly speaking – in this unfrequented wood. Maybe, after all, my wife did have a point.

I watched and waited. Waited and watched. Half the night. I saw nothing; not the whiff of a badger. Baffling. I didn't doubt they were in residence; the signs were clear-cut. Then why their reluctance to oblige? Surely they realized I meant them no harm!

Let me warn you, in case you plan a bit of badger-watching yourself, that success can never be guaranteed. It was many, many months before this was reassuringly brought home to me – reassuringly, because until then I imagined it was entirely my fault for:

Not standing downwind.

Being too near the entrance.

Unconsciously making a noise.

Going back too soon after my initial examination of the sett, with my own scent and my dog's still lingering.

I searched for reasons, demanded them, told myself if I

did this or that differently, disappointment would be a thing of the past. Later I met a real badger authority, a man who not only writes and lectures about them, appears on radio and TV, but gives much of his spare time to supporting his local badger group in practical work to protect badgers. This ranges from encouraging them to move away from potential danger areas (open fields – an invitation to farming antagonism; or private gardens – not universally welcome!) to releasing them from snares and assisting their recovery after road accidents. He astonished me by admitting his own watching of badgers was conspicuously unsuccessful.

'I don't know what it is,' he said. 'Perhaps my scent is particularly pungent or obnoxious to badgers, something of the sort, but I rarely see them. Other people watch, report success. I go to the same sett, and see nothing. Time after time. It's most odd.'

Unfortunately I didn't meet him soon enough. The fiasco at the sett near the heronry was, I believed, entirely my fault – as indeed it probably was – but for the life of me I couldn't see what I'd done wrong.

A retired shepherd in the village, admittedly his own badger-watching a thing of the distant past, told me that beyond doubt the reason was my scent blowing through the sett.

'The breeze swirls,' he said, 'especially in woodland.'

And he went on to say that the best way to monitor this was by hanging a piece of cotton from a tree. My practice was to hold up a handkerchief just before entering the wood, on the assumption the wind would remain constant. I decided to take his advice, though to be honest I've never found it either necessary or possible to change my position once ensconced. In any case, I soon learned that the best viewing position was invariably up a tree, in which situation, swirling wind or not, theoretically my scent should

27

blow well over the sett, beyond reach of even the most sensitive noses.

At the time my only answer to abortive watching was perseverance. If at first you don't succeed . . . And I was determined to succeed. What I'd already seen was enough to counter any suggestion of not trying again.

'Right,' I said to my wife a couple or so days later, 'tonight, two hours before dusk, up the tallest tree handy!'

In truth I found the climbing less than straightforward, and shall refuse to mention grazed shins and torn trousers, too much the story of my life these days. More to the point, I gazed from my elevated station with utter wonderment. Agreed, every gnat in the wood decided to join me, and my excessive fear of making a noise reduced my assaults on them to futility; but the whole situation, never mind the prospect of seeing badgers, was magic, reminiscent of childhood forays into the country with parents who, like me at the time, didn't know one end of a badger from another. I tell you, I was inebriated with happiness. Contentment. Peace and quiet.

Not that the place was quiet for all that long. In broad daylight out trotted not badgers but a vixen and four cubs, precisely where from I couldn't see, but certainly not the entrances under surveillance. I've mentioned badger cubs at play. Fox cubs are little different. They hurled themselves at each other, snarling, wrestling, chasing and gleefully developing hunting skills, casually watched by the vixen, who seemed more concerned to bask in the evening sun than bother with the quarrelling quartet. She stretched herself out as though just finishing a hard day's night, not about to start one. The foxes were no more than twenty strides from the sett, nearer than entrances I knew about whose shape indicated badger possession.

I watched the entertainment for some twenty minutes, intrigued by the energy of all the cubs but most of all by the tiniest, half the size of the others – a runt? – yet capable of sustaining their antics. Almost. Just before they and the vixen disappeared, it broke from the hurly-burly, wandered towards my tree, eventually looked up, gazed at me for ages in disbelief, decided I was harmless and rejoined the group.

Since then a number of badger-watchers have told me that badger cubs too are incredibly tolerant of human company, not given to panic or alarm when discovering observers. I can't go that far, though in my experience they are undoubtedly far less cautious than grown badgers, more given to inquisitiveness than fear.

However, this runt treated my presence with the indifference I hoped for from the badgers. And this time I wasn't disappointed. From the nearest entrance a black and white face appeared; just the face. It sniffed, disappeared, returned to sniff again and waddled into full view.

Soon two . . . five . . . seven badgers were on show – sitting on their backsides as though squaring up to each other, mutually grooming, wrestling, shuffling, stroking their stomachs, probably searching for nits, and one of them fully stretched on its hind legs scratched on *my* tree.

I returned home walking on air, a confirmed badger addict. And I couldn't stop thinking about it – in our badgerless village too!

3

Pig boars and badger boars

Something else I couldn't stop thinking about!

Why are male cows called bulls, male sheep rams, male horses stallions, male foxes dogs; but male pigs *and* badgers boars?

Could it have anything to do with . . . ?

But let me begin at the beginning. Shortly after moving to the country, I found myself involved with sheep – more precisely tupping, that colourful time when randy rams roam the flock seeking out partners in season. It *is* colourful, too, for the rams mark the ewes' backsides with red, blue or yellow raddling powder, indicating to the shepherd which sheep have been served and at what time the lambs are likely to be born.

The mating itself is over in the twinkling of an eye. A quick mount and solitary thrust. Done! No wonder a ram can satisfy fifty sheep – and still be panting for more.

The same quickness applies to a bull serving a cow, though these days he doesn't often get even that moment of glory. Instead the representative from the Milk Marketing Board arrives with sperm from a breed of the farmer's choice, pushes a practised hand up the cow's backside, and promises a second visit if the first proves unsuccessful. It rarely takes long, artificial insemination, but it doesn't compare in speed with a mounting bull.

But pigs!

That's another story altogether. First of all, with pigs, AI is much more difficult; not the technique itself but choosing the right moment. Scientific farming is the answer to many situations, but as yet it hasn't found the answer to knowing precisely when a sow is in season. Unlike the boar! He sniffs and knows unerringly. So the pig farmer, aware the sow is due to come into season, simply leaves the two together and doesn't have to worry further. If he wants ten sows served in a day, the boar will oblige; if only one, she's likely to be served ten times.

Second – and more relevant to my original query – the mating itself is anything but brief. Indeed, the one and only time I witnessed such an event enlightened me as to why 'screwing' is a vulgarism for sexual intercourse. For the end of the boar's penis is shaped like a screw, clearly not without cause, for he screws himself in, and remains blissfully locked for perhaps twenty-five minutes, wallowing with uninhibited and grunting delight. As different from a serving ram or bull as can be imagined.

Incidentally, the fruits of this screwing – farrowing – is inversely proportional, certainly in time and perhaps delight too. Over in a flash. If you blink you've missed the next piglet's arrival. Plop. There it is. And another . . . and another . . . up to ten or eleven, frequently more. But the mating, though as urgent, is, as I say, leisurely, never to be hurried. A man who should know, a lecturer at an agricultural college, told me that each screwing involved a bucket full of semen! I imagine this was nothing more than poetic licence for a considerable amount, but you get the idea. On second thoughts, when I recall seeing that boar at work, perhaps the lecturer was speaking literally!

More to the point, pig boars and badger boars have in common this mating duration. Not that the end of a badger's penis is similarly shaped, as far as I know, but he shares the pig boar's mating athleticism. He shares it without consistently practising it, however, for badgers mate short or long according to the mood. A bit like humans.

The badger boar, again reflecting the pig boar, is also promiscuous, ready to serve more than one sow as opportunity presents itself. Come to that, the sow is no less promiscuous, prepared to be mounted by a couple of boars in quick succession, as long as the senior boar doesn't object. Yet here's the conundrum!

A pig boar serves a sow; and three months, three weeks, three days later – stand by for the farrowing. No variation. Otherwise pig farming would be impossible.

With badgers, it's different. They mate in February, most of them, February to July, though mating is possible much later, even November or early December. Needless to say, I have no personal knowledge of this, rarely having seen a badger under any circumstances from October to early spring. They don't hibernate, but are far less active in colder weather, and – if only because of the fewer hours of daylight – never emerge until well after dark. A few seasoned watchers have infra-red binoculars. Alas, I am relatively unseasoned and not able to afford them.

Nevertheless, the evidence is conclusive that the vast majority of badgers mate in the earlier part of the year; but their cubs are born at approximately the same time, whenever the mating – anything up to twelve months later! You might well wonder, as I did, why the gestation should be so long. I knew about elephants, but this – for such a small animal – was ridiculous.

The retired shepherd put me right. It was, he explained, all to do with a mystery called delayed implantation. The badgers mate, conception takes place, but gestation doesn't immediately – automatically, unstoppably – commence. Why? Apparently no one is absolutely sure. It might be

32

something to do with the weather, food supply, the physical condition of the sow, even, I suppose, her psychological condition, for fear, uncertainty and insecurity can be mighty unconscious deterrents to motherhood. Whatever the reason, the fact remains that badgers are usually impregnated long before the fertilized egg starts to grow. It floats about the uterus, healthy, protected, presumably waiting for the right circumstances to trigger gestation. Then it attaches itself to the uterus wall and begins to develop. Seven or so weeks later, the cubs are born.

Now I know quite a lot about cubs, from watching them at every opportunity to my heart's content. But about the whys and wherefores of this delayed implantation I remain largely in the dark; not terribly concerned, I must admit, not frantic for an explanation. Let the experts, for whom praise be, continue with their research. I am more than content simply to watch the happy outcome of the badgers' mating, five or twenty-five or sixty-five minutes.

4

Badgers, children and ants

I've mentioned the badger-watchers' grapevine. There's also a village grapevine linking virtually every inhabitant, keeping us all in touch with whatever passes for news hereabouts. To be perfectly honest, this fishbowl aspect of village life can be a bit of a trial to newcomers accustomed only to urban anonymity. It isn't that we wish to intrude, least of all to pass on the latest gossip; simply that living in such a small community, far removed from the fleshpots, we find it natural to take a keen neighbourly interest.

Consequently I wasn't altogether surprised – merely shocked – when my interest in badgers became something of a village talking point. My first intimation of this was a friend from the distant past visiting us for the first time since our move to the country. Hopelessly lost in searching for our cottage, finally despairing, he called at the village pub for both sustenance and help.

'You mean the badger man's place!' the barman responded.

Some twenty minutes later he knocked at our door, and immediately expressed interest in my badger-watching, about which, as far as I was aware, he knew nothing.

This grapevine progressively presented its problems. Villagers began not only to ask about the badgers we didn't have in our village, but also to request that I take them with me to watch. You already know, however, that no badger-watcher readily passes on information about the location of setts, even to people he knows and trusts. They talk!

Equally to the point, the more people watching, the less likelihood of the badgers emerging.

So I treated all requests with a measure of reserve, not to say downright denial, until at least convinced that the interest behind them was more than a passing whim. What somewhat complicated this rule was the refusal to take no for an answer by one of my grandchildren. She was all of six, and at times as hyperactive as her eight-year-old brother.

Now don't get me wrong. I was impatient to initiate the pair of them into the delights of badger-watching, never doubting that once they'd seen cubs at play they'd be as addicted as I; but the very idea of needing to be absolutely quiet for an hour or so had immediately changed the elder child's mind. His face had literally dropped at the prospect. The six-year-old wasn't so easily put off. She insisted, contrary to all the evidence, that she could be both still and quiet for as long as necessary.

Wouldn't it be wise, I continued, doing my diplomatic best, to wait till she was a little older?

I realized my cause was lost when some weeks later she told me of a birthday party she'd attended. The hostess introduced a totally new game. First she displayed the prizes, then she explained the rules. Finally she sat the twenty or so children in their places, looked at her watch, and gave the word to start.

There was total silence for twenty unbroken minutes. The miracle game? The three children staying silent the longest were the winners. Ingenious. But also for me confounding, the unanswerable response to my suggestion that the six-year-old wasn't old enough to watch badgers. She won first prize. I hadn't a leg to stand on.

* * *

35

We planned our first joint badger-watching venture with the thoroughness that leaves nothing to chance. Would she be tired staying up so late? Perhaps a little sleep in the afternoon. What to wear? How not to talk, not a word, once we were in the wood. We rehearsed climbing a tree. And, of course, immediately before leaving the cottage – the loo.

We drove to the sett, bubbling with excitement. She was afflicted with proverbial ants in her pants, and I was already worrying that the badgers might not oblige. Disappointing her was unthinkable. The walk from where we left the car to the boundary of the wood was my last opportunity to reiterate the indispensability of silence. Did she understand? A nod bespoke her resolve to keep quiet.

She was, I must admit, remarkably adept for a six-year-old at crawling under the barbed wire holding up the fence, and likewise at stealthily following my footsteps, Good King Wenceslas fashion. With considerable difficulty I climbed the tree, paused to get my breath and reached down for her outstretched hand. In a jiffy she was beside me, settled and gazing at the mammoth entrance. I pointed to confirm this was the area to watch.

For the next two or three minutes I almost forgot she was with me. The stillness, hers most of all! The peace and quiet! In fact I was in a sort of reverie when a tiny voice brought me down to earth, metaphorically speaking, you understand.

A drama in six acts was about to unfold.

Act one

'Grandad.'
  'Shush.'
  'Grandad.'

'You remember,' I whispered, 'what I told you?'

The pause lasted for seconds.

'Grandad.'

I looked down at her pleading eyes.

She confessed, barely audibly, her need to go to the loo.

'Try to wait.' My voice sounded cheerful.

Act two

Two-minute silence.

'Grandad.'

'Shush.'

'I can't wait.'

We whispered our strategy: I would lower her to the foot of the tree. She would tiptoe behind another, perform, and be hauled back, all with the quietness of a mouse.

She reached the ground; took a couple of steps towards the nearest tree; bravely decided that keeping me in her sights was preferable to privacy; squatted; and ensured that enough human scent was awash to warn every badger within miles of our company.

Act three

I hauled her back, wondering whether it was worth staying, not doubting she was bound to be disappointed. Within minutes a sniffing black and white face appeared at the entrance. More sniffing. She pointed and giggled. The face disappeared. Seconds later it was back, with another; and soon we were watching the customary set-to of wrestling, chasing and mutual grooming, unfortunately on the far side of the giant mound.

Act four

From behind our tree appeared first one rabbit then a second, both quickly sitting near the foot of our perch as though for her pleasure. Meanwhile the pair of badgers disappeared to feed. She didn't notice. The rabbits were captivating.

Act five

The rabbits gone, viewing was doubtless over for the night. Then out popped a second pair of badgers, with barely any sniffing, and this time one seemed immediately attracted to our tree. The other followed, and soon we were witnessing almost directly beneath us the whole repertoire of badger antics – wrestling, grooming, scratching, shuffling, and the musking of a sow by a boar from a scent gland above his anus, as he sat on her!

Naturally, after her own ablutions below, she took my later explanation of this in her stride. And I'll tell you something else, too, despite the probability of being thought insufferably romantic, too sentimental by half. If watching badger cubs at play was magic, watching a six-year-old watching badger cubs at play was the best antidote to becoming hard-boiled I'd come across for years.

Finale

I lowered her from the tree, and fell out myself, the pair of us concerned only to withdraw with as little disturbance to the badgers as possible. Once free to talk she couldn't stop, the youngest badger-watching addict of my experience, preoccupied in all her gabbling with a single theme – when could we go again?

That first occasion remains one of the happiest of my badger-watching life. We might not have badgers in our village – but try telling that to this six-year-old visitor from the city. Something else too. She won't tell you where to find the sett!

She *will* tell you, though, all too quickly, what she thinks of me and the ants' nest. Funny thing was, she didn't bat an eyelid when I explained that badgers ate ants as well as wasps and bees, more particularly their pupae and larvae, destroying the entire nest in no time. But this, as far as she was concerned, was somewhat different from my attitude when ants from a nest outside began to invade our cottage on a widening front.

Children, I've discovered, are infuriatingly consistent in their thinking about animals both domestic and wild. Whereas adults, especially ex-townees like me, pontificate about animal rights as pretty well absolute . . . until rat or mouse appears in the garden shed or scullery, wasps set up house near the front door, foxes raid the chickens, moles massacre the lawn, or starlings patronize the bird table intended exclusively for blue tits and the like, children insist that such inconveniences in no way justify terminal retaliation. Adult sophistry cuts no ice!

Her interest in ants was initiated when she, her brother and I came across a nest of incredible activity in the woods. Worker ants were heaving a dead or dying wasp to their food store below ground; a frenzy of co-ordinated purpose, proving that the strength of the whole is infinitely greater than the sum total of its individual parts. We watched spellbound for ages, while I was largely confounded by a barrage of questions.

At another nest in late July, much better prepared, I was able to explain the entirely different frenzied activity –

wingless worker ants falling over each other to bid farewell to the males and females reared in the nest who were flying away to establish nests of their own, mating en route, one queen with perhaps two, three or more males, the latter, having fulfilled their sole function in life, falling to the ground to die.

The females, on the other hand, bursting with promise, each sought a suitable site – a hole in the ground, a tree, a building, or whatever – to develop for the first brood. How? By laying eggs, eating some herself to sustain her own life, then laying more and more, which in turn became pupae, larvae, and finally the three categories of ant – male, female or sexless worker. These very first arrivals were initially sustained by the queen discarding her wings into the soil and adding her own saliva to make a fatty, nourishing paste.

So far so good, though, as you can imagine, my ignorance led to a few hiccups on the way. Undeterred, fired by their inquisitiveness, I spoke of the worker ants existing for the one purpose of serving the males and females to enable them to fulfil their single destiny – the continuance of the line. The workers, inside and outside the nest, toiled non-stop, mindlessly preoccupied, with no thanks, no complaints. No choice.

They fought in defence or attack, collected food and carted it – some among them actually serving as wheelbarrows; others – and this the children found hard to take – functioned as storage tanks, stomachs inflated like barrels with liquid food for hard times; they hung in rows, living containers waiting to be emptied and replenished for the benefit of the community, then cast away like empty bottles when worn out.

The nests themselves were as complicated in design as

any city, with numerous levels, streets, workshops, storerooms, sleeping quarters, nurseries – a maze of ingenuity, everything in place, a place for everything, nothing haphazard or a useless fancy.

What about the fighting? asked the eight-year-old. Did ants use weapons of any sort?

Yes and no, I said. They didn't *use* weapons, they themselves *were* the weapons. According to the minute variation in their bodies and heads and mouths, they were lances, swords, axes, spears; and some of the 3,500 different species of ant were guns, able to fire deadly poison!

By this time, of course, the children's sympathies, never mind their admiration, were all on the side of the workers, especially when I told them that these ants were born into slavery with no possibility of escape or promotion, doomed literally to work themselves to death. The point was underlined as we watched some of them refusing to be discouraged by either the weight of their burden as they dragged, pushed or carried, or my gentle poking of their dead prey. They constantly regrouped, rushed up reinforcements and trampled over each other in their desperation to take their booty underground, interpreting every setback as a call to greater effort. Incredible creatures. Miracles of the commonplace.

So when they extended their empire to our cottage we weren't overconcerned. The few we saw at first actually added to the children's interest and pleasure. The six-year-old picked one up, or rather allowed it to climb on to her hand, and kept it scurrying by replacing a palm each time the boundary of the other was reached; not unlike running on the spot. The ant was tireless, arousing her merriment. Finally it was returned to the entrance to the nest with a tenderness usually reserved for the new-laid eggs she collected from our half-dozen hens.

Then, almost before we knew what was happening, the ants bored or found a hole leading indoors and spread themselves on an alarming scale. Something clearly had to be done. Quickly. Yes, but what, exactly? The children found the ants more fascinating than troublesome. Arguments that they were inconvenient and certain soon to invade the kitchen made no impression at all.

All this, however, was before the entire nest of unsuspected proportions began to mass prior to the next nuptial flight! We watched, children and neighbours too, with a degree of awe and anxiety. Within the swarming, frenzied mass, wings were prematurely shed or knocked off; either way, the result was an unbelievable mess.

There could be only one outcome. I applied an instant killer spray and washed away the corpses plus lingering survivors with scalding water.

It only remains for me to report that the children continue to be nothing less than perverse in their remembrance of the massacre, every time I mention the importance of conservation.

Better stick to badger-watching, about which the pair of them – for soon the eight-year-old proved that he too possessed this unlikely capacity for sustained quietness – had no reservations; the very opposite.

By now I had discovered four active setts, plus another I couldn't make up my mind about. Was it active? More crucially, were there badgers in that area at all? Sometimes I thought one thing, sometimes another. I couldn't find any dung pits or tree scratchings; and the paths looked barely used. Yet surely the entrances indicated badgers? On second thoughts, perhaps foxes? It wasn't so immediately straightforward for a relative novice.

I'd watched towards dusk only once, spotting a fox in

the distance nonchalantly staring in my direction, not a badger to be seen long after dark when I withdrew. Nevertheless, the thought wouldn't go away. There could be badgers! And in a part of the woods which until then I thought I knew like the back of my hand. What compounded my refusal to accept all contrary evidence was a casual remark by a woman living on the boundary of the woods. She told me that she and her husband were pretty sure badgers were about, not all that far from their cottage, but to watch at night was too eerie for comfort.

I knew the feeling. Just occasionally, the trees, as I've mentioned, look menacing; and once this sort of nonsense gets a hold, one's imagination is fearsomely creative! What normally charms, like falling leaves making music or trees suggesting their identity with distinctive sighs in the wind or the merest sound of bird or wild animal, becomes a threat, an ominous approach, a prelude to the unthinkable.

I remember talking this over with a man who'd worked in the woods all his life. He'd never seen a badger, for the simple reason he'd never been in the woods at night! During the day, he could think of no lovelier environment in which to labour. But the very idea of returning at night . . .

Actually, what sparked off our conversation was an official form he'd received notifying him that to work alone in the woods was against the law. Day or night. Either he employed an assistant, not needed or wanted, or went out of business.

'Don't make sense,' he said. 'I've worked in these woods for nigh thirty years, no trouble; now all of a sudden this arrives.' He held out the form for me to see.

'I suppose it's in case you have an accident or something, and need help with no one to hand; could that be it?' I asked.

'Ain't happened in thirty years,' he smiled. 'No reason to think it's more likely now.'

I mentioned his problem to my wife, and uncharacteristically she was on the side of the bureaucrats.

'Makes sense to me,' she said. 'I keep asking myself where and how I'd find you, if anything happened as you prowled around. Where to begin looking? Half the time I don't even know which sett you're watching, always supposing I could find my way in the dark if I did!'

I was to remember her words at a moment of triumphant ineptitude, miles from anywhere or anyone, blood flowing like beer at an Irish wake; but details must wait. Of far more concern at the time was our need temporarily to leave our badgerless village for a part of the country I didn't know, a part possibly really devoid of badgers.

I needn't have worried.

5

An elusive countryman

Our new setting was a farm cottage on the outskirts of a hamlet, in wild, beautiful terrain surrounded by hills, as unlike Kent as is possible to imagine. The farmer showed me where to find wood to be chopped for our stove. I picked up the axe.

'Any badgers in this area?' I asked as he turned to leave what resembled a converted cowshed.

He led me outside, pointed to woodland some half a mile away as the crow flies, and said he thought, he'd heard from somewhere, about a sett reputedly there. Not on his land. The next farm! Nice chap, the farmer. Mark you, he hadn't seen the sett personally, only heard about it. But he supposed it must be there because he'd known rumours about it for years.

At the first opportunity, I knocked on the neighbouring farmer's door, unmistakably the *back* door hidden away down the side of the farmhouse. A garden gate leading to the front door carried a notice: *No entry*. I knocked again. No one in. Time, I thought, to search for a reservoir beauty spot comfortably within walking distance before I knocked again. But I didn't get very far. Up the road a young woman, baby in pram nearby, was working in the garden. She smiled. We talked. I wondered whether she'd heard of the badger sett? No, not at that farm, she said. But up the next turning, a narrow lane, some of it desperately in need of repair, leading past two or three cottages, there was a man who was sure to know. He lived at the sort of crossroads, a white cottage, a mile at most. 'You can't miss it,' she concluded.

I knocked on *his* door. Again no answer. A man was pottering in a garden up the road, his married daughter's, as he soon told me.

'Badgers!' he replied to my enquiry, 'I have heard yon wood's the place to look; not that I know at first hand; never seen a badger in my life, more's the pity. No time. They come out only at night, don't they?'

I admitted this was usual, adding that daytime sightings weren't unknown. He looked unconvinced and assured me they came out only at night in this area. He told me authoritatively that the person who knew all about badgers, everything there was to know, lived in a white cottage at the crossroads.

'He's not in,' I said.

'Never is,' he laughed. 'Funny bloke. Lives alone with his dog; roam all over the place, they do. You might find him in the betting shop.'

He paused, waiting for the imagined bombshell to register.

'But *he*'s the man for wildlife,' he continued. 'Listen, what Larry doesn't know about badgers and foxes, that sort of thing, isn't worth knowing. You ought to talk with him.'

I made my way back to the farmhouse, my original port of call, immediately heartened by a van parked outside. There was no need to knock. As I approached the back door, the farmer and his wife, eating a late lunch in the kitchen, spotted me through a window.

'Badgers!' he smiled.

'I'll come back,' I said, 'when it's more convenient.'

'Come in,' called his wife. 'Come in.'

And in I went.

Now there are occasions when a welcome is, as they say

up north, more felt than telt. Know what I mean? The words might be mumbled, stumbled over, monosyllabic; but their warmth cannot be doubted. More, their very incoherence eloquently communicates both pleasure and interest. Such was the case during the next five minutes. We nattered like old pals, quickly exchanged personal pedigrees, and told each other that badgers were deserving of every consideration.

Yes, they did have a sett – the farmer and his wife made no attempt to hide their pride – in the spinney across the field with a pylon. He pointed to the place and told me it had been there for years.

'Follow the path,' he said. 'Bear slightly left at the pylon, and enter the spinney at the corner. You'll find the badgers, plenty of 'em. Call in on your way back,' he urged as I left them to finish their lunch.

I knew all about country hospitality, but this really was something else!

The corner proved to be overgrown with giant blackberry runners, nettles and thistles. I followed the barbed wire, and slipped under a loose piece. The ground was smothered with wood anemones and bluebells, the main reason why I didn't doubt that badgers were about, for paths of flattened stems, suggestive of tunnels, unmistakably confirmed I'd found the right place. And the more I followed them, searching for entrances, the greater became my excitement.

Here was a text-book sett, all the indicators clearly evident in abundance: not only paths throughout the entire spinney, with clusters of entrances, others single or in pairs dotted here and there, dung pits, scratched trees, play areas and fresh digging, but also bedding left to air at an entrance with a massive mound of excavated earth, something I'd seen only once before. So they really did bring the straw, leaves and other ingredients of their sleeping quarters above ground to freshen up.

In retrospect, I shouldn't have been so surprised; but as I gazed with something akin to awe, I thought how incredibly human it looked. Badger bedding hanging out to dry! Truth to tell, I have since come across a degree of friendly agnosticism about this interpretation of bedding material at entrances. Some authorities have no doubts; others have yet to be convinced. And superficially it does seem strange that badgers should take the trouble to air old bedding when a plentitude of renewal is invariably to hand. Ah, yes, but we all know how bedding is personal and intimate, illustrated, for instance, by a farmer I know giving a handful of straw from the whelps' nursery to each buyer of a sheepdog puppy, his argument being that this will help the puppy to settle in its new home. There's nothing like sleeping in your own bed!

Anyhow, I saw this roll of straw at the entrance, at the top of the mound, and immediately assumed it was bedding being aired. Nearby was a huge oak tree with a hollow of branches from the trunk some eight feet up, and convenient foot and hand holds to haul myself up: the most perfect hide. All I needed to do now was return an hour or so before dusk, allowing at least twenty-four hours for my scent to disperse.

In the event, I made arrangements to watch on the following day. The farmer and his wife appeared to be as excited at the prospect as I, and it was only then they confessed: despite being bought up in the country and living at their present farm for many years, they'd never actually seen a badger. Not one. Ever. The farmer laughed as he told me. His wife sounded apologetic. I commiserated. They explained that life was so busy, especially in the summer, when badgers were most co-operative about showing themselves. How many times had he said to his wife, and she to him, that they must go to the spinney to see for themselves. 'But you know how it is . . .'

I did. Almost. For it struck me as strange that such deep-dyed country people with badgers relatively on their own doorstep could resist the opportunity.

From their farmhouse to my selected tree took no more than minutes. By a little after seven-fifteen, a good two hours before dusk, I was snugly ensconced. The view was breathtaking: a carpet of rich blue with suggestions of white and purple from the fading anemones; splashes of yellow from primroses and lesser celandine in brilliant clusters, the whole scene etching itself on my mind like an idealized portrait of woodland in late spring.

As usual, the silence beneath silence slowly seeped into my very soul; *beneath* because the surface silence was anything but, full of scurrying rabbits, twittering birds, a circling colony of rooks (for what purpose I failed to see), roosting pigeons, the inevitable crows cawing protest – possibly about my unwanted company, cracking and tremor in the undergrowth and other noises of the wood I couldn't make out. And a movement outside the spinney. Getting nearer. Badgers already? From an entrance beyond my vision?

The approach from the top end of the spinney was clearly in the direction of my tree. I strained my eyes, feeling elated at my good fortune. I confidently expected at least one black and white face to swing into view. Instead, I saw two faces coming through the trees, nearer and unbelievably nearer.

The farmer and his wife!

I didn't know what to do. If they came any closer they'd put paid to badger-watching for the night. Yet if I called out, told them of their unintended sabotage . . . On the other hand, if I didn't . . .

By now they were clearly in view, mystified they couldn't find me, intrigued, provoked to animation at my evaporation. He glanced around, puzzled. His wife neared the mound, fascinated by the bedding, loudly wondering about the digging of new earth, debating with her husband about the cause. Baiters? The dread did nothing to keep her feet – and scent – off the vital area.

I looked down unbelievingly, affronted they wanted to trample their own spinney. Just when I . . .

I grunted. That's right, like a pig. I couldn't think of any better way of attracting their attention without indicating my scary presence to the badgers doubtless already wondering below. I grunted again. They looked up, amazed, only half sure what I was up to, and smiled a greeting that rapidly faded. For my face positively registered both exasperation and unwelcome. Unmistakably, shamelessly, my eyes told them to get the hell out of it!

They did, graciously, not wasting a moment, leaving me with my embarrassment and regret and guilt. What a way to say thank you for their ready permission and helpfulness!

Dusk, like my self-recrimination, began to deepen.

A black and white face sniffed the air, disappeared, came into fuller view, then finally emerged completely, still suspicious, however. Never mind the possibility of alien scent, perhaps my tree was too close, somehow communicating my presence to the badger's sixth sense.

It snuffled near the entrance, seemed undecided, ventured a little further, eventually nearer my tree, and finally made off casually in the opposite direction, clearly not alarmed. Minutes passed. Twilight thickened. Was this, I wondered, the extent of my viewing for the night? Peering into the darkness, I resolved that next time I'd find a perch more reasonably distanced. Better safe than sorry. I felt for my torch and was about to switch it on to assist my descent, when – *wallop*, out of nowhere, certainly not from the entrance I was watching, a veritable avalanche of badgers. Ten in all, yes, *ten*, the largest number at that time I'd ever seen all together. They flounced around, seemingly engaged in a communal game, then three of them – sows, judging by their size – broke off to snuffle, the rest continuing their playful antics.

The first badger returned and joined in the fun, then four more from my entrance, a total of fifteen gallivanting like crazy. Frankly it was hard to believe the evidence of my own eyes. The average sett is thought to contain less than half this number. Furthermore, though this was the time for the emergence of cubs, the members of this group were well past that stage. So with these fifteen *and* the cubs, how many occupied the spinney?

The darkness was now almost impenetrable; futile for me to hang about. But the badgers were still active near my tree. If I suddenly descended they'd be scared out of their wits, and doubtless made more wary the next time I watched. I could, of course, have switched on the torch, fitted with a red filter for such an occasion, but I didn't want to risk it, not this first time at the sett, not after such a magnificent display. My one concern now was to creep away without disturbing the badgers.

Then I remembered something I'd read by, I think, Ernest Neal, patron saint of badger-watchers virtually the world over (*The Natural History of Badgers*, Ernest Neal, Croom Helm, 1986). He suggested that in this sort of situation the best way to withdraw was first to make a clicking noise with the tongue, just loud enough for the badgers to hear without alarm.

51

It worked.

They stopped playing. Unsure, they looked in my direction. And scarpered, all but three or four. These bravest, including two boars, kept looking and sniffing.

I clicked again.

That did it!

The way was now clear for me to leave my tree and negotiate the barbed wire.

En route for the car in the farmyard, I decided to put off reporting to the farmer and his wife until the next day. Well, it *was* late, despite the farmhouse kitchen being ablaze with light; and anyway I needed to apologize rather than merely report, an act of contrition better offered, I convinced myself, unhurriedly in the full light of day. Of such rationalization is cowardice made. As things turned out, the farmer and his wife brushed aside my regrets, told me they should have known better, and repeated their resolve to watch the badgers themselves. Soon.

I left them to return to the sett, impatient to locate the entrance or entrances from which the avalanche of badgers had descended, for I too was resolved to watch soon, that night if possible, lingering scent or not. Following the direction from which they'd appeared out of nowhere, I found more entrances, a couple of them adjacent, two more about six or eight strides apart. The best watching point nominated itself – a fallen tree sufficiently in leaf to offer both cover and comfort.

Once more I returned to the farmhouse.

'If ever you find time to go badger-watching,' I said, 'the best place is not where you saw me last night, but from a fallen tree just inside the spinney near the corner by the pylon.'

And to this spot I made my own way well before dusk.

* * *

Now one of the bonuses of badger-watching, believe me, is this waiting time, to the uninitiated a bore, to insiders full of movement and the unexpected. On this occasion – forget the playful rabbits and cawing crows and chattering magpies – I was tantalized by movement I couldn't understand. Much too early, I thought, for badgers. Too heavy for smaller mammals like wood mice or voles. Yet it persisted, driving me mad with curiosity.

I strained to see.

Nothing.

Only the noise.

Then, trotting down a badger path leading almost directly to my tree, came a fox cub, definitely a *cub*, though mysteriously alone. It sniffed, looked around in apparent wonderment, and advanced warily on one of the entrances I was watching; more sniffing, and it trotted out of sight.

I was disappointed, maybe for the wrong reason. For even as it briefly explored the entrance, I wondered what would happen if a badger emerged. Would it go for the fox cub? I've already mentioned that generally badgers and foxes tolerate each other with no suggestion of animosity. True, a fox was once seen to kill a badger or at least cause its death in a fight; and there are records the other way round, enough to indicate that badgers, with their steel claws and teeth, are far more likely to emerge victorious in such conflicts. Normally, however, they happily co-exist.

None the less the majority of fox and badger cubs are born at about the same time – February – and a badger sow can be awesomely fierce if she suspects her cubs are threatened. Whereas in such a situation a vixen might make off, not heedless of her cubs but laying a scent to divert the attacker from them, a badger sow would almost certainly fight. To the death, one way or the other, if needs be.

The motives of an innocent fox cub poking around at an entrance with badger cubs inside might be misunderstood!

I suppose it was, in fact, some thirty minutes later that the first black and white face showed itself, for a sniffing second or two, no more. Then out popped the first of three cubs, followed by the sow. And did they immediately give her a hard time! Like naughty children let out to play, with too much energy from being cooped up for too long, they chased, dived, rolled, wrestled, snarled and pestered, granting their mother not a moment's respite. At times she resembled someone fleeing a swarm of bees on the warpath. The essential difference was that her fleeing was unmistakably a game, fun, hilarious for all involved, including herself. She ran away, leaped over her pursuers as she backtracked, rolled in the bluebells, let the cubs jump all over her, pushed them off, welcomed them back, ran again – a cycle of merriment.

And I wasn't the only one watching!

The fox cub suddenly returned like a hunter, nose forward, tail down, body crouched very low. Mystified, I think. It crept forward barely perceptibly, its eyes riveted on the flailing heads and legs and bodies, its ears pricked at the squeals and squeaks. Closer. Closer.

The furious fun continued, spasmodically quickening. Surely the sow was conscious of the fox cub's presence? If she was, she ignored it totally, preoccupied with her rampaging cubs. But there was a sudden change in the cubs' game, though, on reflection, it couldn't have been the fox cub that caused it. One moment they were all over the sow, the next tearing off in pursuit of each other, straight for the fox cub. It didn't hang about! Like the proverbial scalded cat, it shot off, either ignored or unnoticed by the badger cubs, all three too occupied in knocking the living daylights out of their new victims – each other.

Meanwhile the sow wandered off in the *opposite* direction and disappeared, for all the world as though the safety of her cubs was the least of her concerns. And long after the fox cub had disappeared too, her cubs continued to play like man-eating lions over a solitary prey. How they came to no harm puzzled me. On second thoughts, perhaps they did actually hurt each other, part of their learning how to use claws and teeth for the serious business of independent survival.

It brought to mind a farmer who told me of trying to snare a fox, and – like his counterpart who owned the wood with the heronry – trapping a badger. The development caused not only acute distress (he meant the badger no harm) but a subsequent problem – how to release it? His slightest approach sent the captured animal into a frenzy, its claws like its teeth underlining the wisdom of keeping well clear.

What to do? Knock it out with one mighty blow, and cut the snare before the badger regained consciousness? The idea appalled him. Which was no doubt commendable but still left him with the captured badger, the snare cutting into its neck, deeper and deeper as it struggled to get away at his approach. Being a sensitive man, he shared its desperation.

One of his workers came up with a suggestion. Badgers, he said, have special jaws that can't be dislocated no matter how hard they bite. Why not let this one bite on an axe handle, throw a sack over its head at the same time, pin it down at the neck with an old-fashioned hayfork and snip the wire?

Why not indeed!

The badger bit; the sack was thrown; the hayfork pinned; the snare was cut. Not, it's true, without a degree of difficulty, but it all worked, and the badger scampered away, no encouragement needed, leaving behind an axe handle in two pieces. Fearsome biters, badgers!

Incidentally, he dealt with the foxes without using snares, his detestation of the vixen and her mate, like his determination to get rid of them, quickened by their growing audacity. Daytime raids increased, the wily creatures' answer to his meticulous care in locking the henhouses well before dusk and keeping them locked until after breakfast. Everywhere he went on the farm he took his shotgun; by car, tractor, Land Rover, or on foot, it made no difference – his gun stayed within easy reach. In theory. The day came when he actually saw a fox with a hen in its mouth, saw it as clear as could be from the tractor, reached for his gun – and realized he'd forgotten it.

He didn't forget it again, especially after this marauding fox, presumably accustomed to seeing both tractor and driver without a hint of danger, appeared to mock his impotence. It simply trotted away, cocking its brush to his threats and curses, seemingly challenging his right to complain not only about the hen in its mouth but about the countless others similarly taken.

'Right, you bugger!' he whispered.

Once more, this time in the farmyard itself, the fox contemptuously glanced at the tractor, confident it represented no danger. *Bang*. It had taken its last hen.

'Got the surprise of its life.' He beamed with satisfaction in the telling. 'Bloody fox. And it wasn't long,' he chuckled, 'before its mate went the same way.' He paused, reliving the moment. 'Now badgers' – he sounded benign – 'they're no trouble. Not here, anyway. No trouble at all. We like 'em on the place. But foxes!' He spat out his feelings. 'They're a different proposition; can't abide 'em. Vermin. That's all they are.'

*　*　*

56

Vermin or not, this fox cub in the spinney looked the extreme opposite. And the farmer and his wife, having no hens, were charmed when I told them about it and the badger cubs. On the spot, their resolve to watch at the spinney, renewed, reinforced, was made to sound like a matter of life and death.

'Come back any time you like,' they said. 'Any time! By the way, do you ever go for a drink at the Royal Oak?'

I confessed my addiction to the ploughman's lunch.

'Nice pub,' he said. 'We go there sometimes ourselves. Not often.' He looked at me hard and smiled shyly. 'You really ought to talk to Larry about badgers; at the cross-roads, the white cottage. What he doesn't know about badgers . . .'

It was like hearing a record played for the umpteenth time.

6

Larry at last

If the truth were known, I'd already returned to that white cottage half a dozen times; and another half a dozen proved necessary, finally, I suspect, for more than my interest in badgers. Larry's elusiveness had become a challenge in itself, something against which to pit my tenacity; just to locate him, prove my determination not to be beaten, triumph over his bloody-mindedness always to be out when I called. It wasn't that I doubted his existence. How could I, with so many people talking about him, urging me to meet him?' But my inability to catch him in assumed cat-and-mouse proportions.

And eventually, as night follows the day of empty-headed persistence, my knocking was answered by this Welsh Scarlet Pimpernel. He blinked, rubbing his eyes as though requiring confirmation I or anybody else was there, told his dog to shut up, and stepped out into his patch of front garden, a veritable wilderness in contrast, I was soon to discover, to the ordered vegetable acre or so at the back.

Yes, he was interested in badgers.

No, he wasn't often in. Being self-employed, he went here, there and everywhere, digging gardens, mowing lawns, catching moles, thinning woodland, building hedges, chopping logs, shearing, haymaking – or, rather, silage-making these days – anything as required. Plenty of work, he said, more than he wanted, some regular, most casual, depending on the time of the year.

'What do *you* do?' he asked, abruptly but not offensively, the countryman's way of seeking credentials from a stranger. I told him; and naturally went on to underline my recent and growing interest in badgers.

'Badgers!' He smiled broadly, looking me up and down. 'What do you know about badgers?' His voice was unmistakably teasing, again not offensive but not entirely free of scepticism either. Clearly my townee background was obvious to this man born and bred in the country.

I admitted I didn't know much, adding that by all accounts he was vastly knowledgeable. And I wondered whether he could put some of his local expertise at my disposal!

Now I don't want to give the impression that within minutes, at this first or even the second meeting, we were chatting like old friends. In my experience this isn't the way the vast majority of countrymen react to newcomers, especially if, like Larry, they live and often work alone, virtually see no one for days and weeks at a time. Hardly talkative types! No, they do a lot of listening, get to know you, satisfy themselves you're trustworthy – meaning not likely to do them down. Normally it doesn't take a day longer than a century or two.

But Larry was different in lots of ways, not least in dropping his guard and taking me into his confidence about far more than badgers. Moles were his first love; in itself quite a paradox, for it transpired that he'd worked for more years than he cared to remember as a mole-catcher; he'd killed thousands, he said, in his time. Thousands! Yet still he loved these little creatures, perhaps admired rather than loved, though either way there was no doubting the involvement of his emotions.

To illustrate their prowess as diggers, he told me that frequently, in the seconds between being located and 'removed', not a few manage to excavate an escape. 'Their claws,' he said, 'are more efficient than mechanical diggers, and they are capable of incredible speed, their forelegs as effective as pneumatic drills. They create their own larder,' he explained, 'filling it with worms paralysed by a judicious bite. Ask any badger,' he laughed. 'They'll tell you; not averse to plundering a mole's larder; take advantage of all the little fella's hard work; scoff the lot in no time; never, though' – and here he paused – 'never, though, the mole itself.

'I don't kill 'em now,' he went on, 'don't kill at all, almost nothing, not these days. Perhaps I'm getting soft as I grow older.' His leather face bespoke embarrassment.

He told me he'd started killing as a lad, with a catapult. Crack shot he was, able to knock sparrows and the like from branch or clothes-line at a goodly distance. One day, he reminisced, he was walking near a farmyard, his catapult swinging behind his back. All of a sudden he felt a pain in his hand, turned round sharp and saw a cockerel about to attack again.

In one practised movement, he loaded and let fly, not stopping to think. Only as the cockerel lay at his feet breathing its last did he realize the magnitude of what he'd done – dispatched the farmer's pride and joy – and the inevitable consequences. For this cockerel was special, winner at local shows, as much its owner's pet as indispensable to his reputation and his hens.

What to do? Confess? Offer to pay for the unbuyable? Say he was sorry? Larry appeared once more caught up in his boyhood dilemma, as though still needing to make a decision, confronted by the unbelievable and its retribution. His eyes twinkled. He chuckled. Laughed. Couldn't contain his merriment at the remembrance. 'What do you think I did?' he nearly choked. My silence conveyed my cluelessness. 'All I did' – he lingered over each word – 'all I did was pluck a few feathers, enough to give the impression

I wanted, scatter them on a trail from farmyard to hedge; and bury the corpse where it wouldn't be found.

'It worked! The farmer blamed a fox. Never did find out. Didn't even suspect.'

By now this normally reserved man was beside himself. 'Phew, it was a near thing!' He struggled for the words to surface from his paroxysm of innocent gloating. And if I say that this simple picture accurately reflects Larry the lad some fifty years later, you have the measure of the man. As shrewd as empty of guile. In fact, he's about the finest example of a simple countryman I've met. Simple? Not intellectually; he won a scholarship to grammar school. Not in terms of naïvety; he's vastly experienced, all there, wide awake. Only simple in the sense of being straightforward, as open as a book, pure in heart, free of the concerns and priorities that bother most of us. If you mention the rat race to Larry, he'll probably tell you about the rat that ran over his bare foot when he was about two years old, on his way from bed to outside lavatory, and terrified him into speechlessness for days, leaving a permanent speech impediment.

That rat, he believes, affected his whole life. At grammar school, for instance, he knew the answers, knew them as well as any of the other boys with hands raised; but he never raised his, not once, afraid that if invited to respond, his stutter would make him sound a fool, an object of mockery. Hardly surprisingly he hates rats, always has from that distant memory, but not any longer to the extent of wanting to kill them. Slayer of thousands of moles, not to mention other animals, he might have been, with cata-pult, traps, snares or gun, but these days he prefers to watch, observe, understand, enjoy. Even rats! A gentle man in the truest sense.

Perhaps in nothing more than his attitude to dogs.

A wise old countryman once told me never to let a dog smell my fear of it, otherwise the dog, not I, would dominate. With Larry it was, it seemed to me, somewhat different. He never needed to camouflage his fear in the face of a fierce or threatening dog. He never had any, not a trace. Unhesitatingly he walked up to it, addressing it softly all the time, reaching out a hand of friendship. Invariably the dog stopped growling and started to wag its tail.

In truth, Larry was averse to barking dogs. Not that he objected to such natural canine behaviour, but he believed that most barkers reflected badly on their owners.

'There's barking and barking,' he used to say, 'natural and unnatural, happy and miserable. Mark my word,' he summed up, 'wherever you find a dog that barks at anybody and everybody approaching, you can be sure it's not treated right.' And by *not treated right* he only meant not spoken to often enough in tones of affection.

One thing was soon beyond dispute. My dog loved to see Larry. Within seconds of his sitting down in our cottage, she would nestle beside him, and he would knead her ears, spasmodically whispering sweet nothings into them. He paid her attention throughout, as unselfconsciously as country wisdom marked his sparse comments.

A remarkable man! He could turn his hand, as I've indicated, to pretty well any ancient craft, yet significantly was as poor as a church mouse. Whenever I think of Larry I wonder at the way we undervalue or underpay craftsmen of his calibre. To be fair, part of the blame is his own refusal to change his business habits. He fixes the price according to the circumstances of his customers. And quite a few of them, ageing widows no longer able to manage their own gardens, finding it increasingly difficult to make ends meet, *depend* upon him, and pay him nearly the same as when he started.

'If I put the price up,' he explains, 'they wouldn't be able to afford it, and then what would they do?' For a man like Larry, there is, as we say, no answer to that!

But let me get back to our very first meeting. His knowledge about badgers, my primary interest, the reason for my persistent knocking on his door, quickly became self-evident, as did his information regarding local setts, one in particular about which he enthused. Not that he was very forthcoming. I was a stranger. Before passing on precise details, he wanted to be sure I was trustworthy, something I appreciate far more now, sharing his excessive caution in like circumstances.

He mentioned his own badger-watching, of taking a lad in the village to a sett, and his gratification at the thirteen-year-old's reaction to his first sighting; of guiding a photographer friend, and their joint amazement at the speed with which the badgers adjusted to the flash, finally ignoring it altogether. He talked about badger mannerisms, mating, cubs, compared the strength of badger claws with those of his favourite wild animal – the mole – and discussed how long before dusk it was wise to arrive for watching, insisting my two hours was much too long or unnecessary (something about which we still disagree); but about pinpointing the setts he said not a word. He did, however, promise to check a sett he thought I might find interesting, and to let me know!

I never doubted that he would, one way or the other. For I left him certain of nothing more than his honesty. He wasn't the type of man to say one thing and mean another, or promise the earth to save the embarrassment of refusal. So when, within days, a message arrived telling me to be ready early evening the day after tomorrow, he'd call for me, I wasn't a bit surprised. But I was absolutely astonished at what I discovered at the sett.

It wasn't so much the sett itself, though intertwining elder trees on either side of the main entrances, creating what resembled a cave or tunnel, made it unique in my experience. Rather it was the preparation made for my visit. For Larry, assisted, I gathered, by one of his sons, had carefully cleared sufficient nettles and thistles for watching at the only point possible. The amount of work! I couldn't believe it.

Together we examined the sett and environs, found a way through the cavern of trees to a steep bank and into a field of grass soon to be cut for silage, some of it flattened – doubtless by the badgers – and circled back to the watching point. There was another snag. This one place for viewing was in a field on the near side of the sett, a field fenced with barbed wire running along the top, and containing some twenty Friesians whose inquisitiveness at our presence rapidly developed into an ardent wish for intimacy. Not that they were mildly aggressive, let alone dangerous – the very opposite, by the way, of any Friesian *bull* you might come across. Be warned! Never trust Jersey, Guernsey or Friesian bulls. Come to think of it, never trust bulls at all, though an Angus, a Hereford, a Galloway, or a Charolais – a veritable colossus – is as cuddly as a bear – but I never have believed that bears are entirely cuddly.

Never mind, these Friesian cows were the opposite of unfriendly, jostling to share our limited area, flush against the fence, sticking their noses over, urinating like waterfalls where we hoped to stand, and generally seeking to endear themselves. Naturally we didn't stay long. Larry never intended that we should, not with our scent, besides the recent disturbance of nettles and thistles, to encourage every self-regarding badger to stay below. But even he hadn't reckoned on the stampeding Friesians.

I returned alone about a week later, not – as with Larry – part of the way by car, but on foot as near as possible as the crow flies. It was some fifteen minutes from our cottage. Barbed wire on the far side of the silage field required negotiating. I cocked my leg over with due circumspection, and too late discovered that the ground on the other side sloped sharply, leaving me too committed, one leg on either side of the fence, the barbs searching for at least my crutch, my trousers firmly hooked. Struggling to unhook myself, I lost my footing on the sloping side, nearly did myself a mischief, and finished up hanging on to the barbed wire as resolutely as the barbed wire was hanging on to me. With commendable presence of mind I heaved myself free of the barbs and cocked over my other leg, all in one slick movement, but lost my footing and went down with a wallop, hitting my nose, leaving too much of it on a barb, seeing stars and wondering why it was suddenly decidedly draughty in the region of the aforementioned crutch.

Blood was all over the place, from hands, nose, other more delicate areas, dripping on my trousers, the flow barely stemmed by my whiter than white handkerchief. At least I'd fallen *into* the field, en route for the sett! And standing there, the draught now feeling like a gale, I couldn't help but laugh at my predicament. How to get home without too much exposure? But first, what about the watching?

My arrival at the sett, the one point for observation, proved irresistible to the Friesians. They came straight over, warned every badger within miles of my presence, and engaged, far too many of them, in what I can perhaps most sensitively describe as co-ordinated bowel evacuation. I realized then that this was no time for the faint-hearted. Better to get out of here before more than my trousers demanded rearguard attention.

The next night, undeterred, I returned, greeted once more rapturously by the jostling Friesians. Don't get me wrong. I love Friesians; we have a herd behind our cottage in Kent, and their spasmodic bulling is the kind of music I expect to hear in the next world too. But these twenty-odd scrummed down within strides of my restricted area. While I silently shooed, they thunderously shoved. The badgers must have wondered about the excessive vibrations plus, of course, the noise.

At last the jostlers wandered off to chew the cud, leaving me only the flies excited by the latest cowpats. I was further encouraged by a rabbit, presumably accustomed to the herd, hopping in my direction, finally almost near enough to be touched. At least someone wasn't aware of my presence!

Time flashed by. And a little after nine, well before dusk, a badger stuck its head from an entrance, sniffed, and apparently decided all was not well. My only glimpse of the night. Somewhat disappointed, but not entirely surprised, I decided not to hang about. The Friesians were again gathering for another charge, my nose was tender, not unlike a few invisible parts of my person, and I thought it best to negotiate the offending barbed wire while it was still light.

Walking round the hayfield was hard work. The grass was long, ready for cutting to be made into silage. Have you noticed, by the way, how traditional haymaking is virtually a thing of the past? You'll see very little these days of cutting and leaving to dry and fluffing up and baling and carting to the barn for stacking, even less of the once ubiquitous hayfork and haystack. Whatever the weather, incredible machines now cut the hay, roll it into giant cylinder shapes, wrap them in airtight polythene and leave them piled in the fields conveniently to hand for winter nourishment. The animals go berserk over it, like children with syrup. There is, I gather, another way of making silage – chopping the hay into short pieces and mixing them with an additive – but the farmers I know, struggling to survive against giant takeovers, are happy with the unchopped. For a start, it's much cheaper for their requirements; and nothing is more decisive than finance, what with milk quotas and surplus mountains and shrinking, if not disappearing, grants. But all this, as I say, is by the way.

I was trudging the hayfield on my way home, lost in thought, when a movement caught my eye. I glanced and froze. A badger? Four badgers! Their black and white faces peered over the hay in my direction. Cubs. Not sure whether I was friend or foe. One decided to take no chances. The others continued to look at me, overcame their inclination to scarper, and returned to their snuffling. I nearly laughed out loud at their indifference to my company. Indeed, I probably did make a noise, for suddenly one was off, followed by the remaining two, to adjacent woodland. Briefly I poked around, saw plenty of paths or runs, and decided to return next day for unhurried inspection.

To locate the sett was easy; it was not far from where I'd watched the cubs disappear from the field. But what about all these other paths leading further up the field and into the same woodland – not a wood, rather a strip of trees and undergrowth – some two hundred strides from the entrances I'd discovered? I followed them with the ease of reading a map and came to one cluster of entrances after another, all of them with the usual indicators of badger occupation. A main sett, with an outlier for a sow and the four cubs? There was only one sure way of finding out. My wife agreed to come with me, to get her first eyeful of badger cubs. And not only cubs! For she was yet to see her first badger other than one scampering across the road in the car lights, all over literally in a flash. Not that she hadn't tried, having accompanied me to a sett in Kent, only to trail home with greater understanding of why the rumour persisted that we had no badgers in our village.

There's a strange thing about taking the uninitiated to watch badgers. I noticed it the first time a couple of city friends, mad keen to catch their first glimpse, came with me to a sett I'd carefully chosen because of my own consistent good fortune in watching there. As the badgerless minutes ticked by, I began to feel not only responsible for their disappointment, but guilty, as though my very integrity was in doubt. After all, what proof was there – apart from my word – tht badgers were in residence at all?

Now here was my wife agreeing to try again, agreeing with what I can only describe as reluctant enthusiasm; keen to come, reconciled to seeing nothing.

As we neared the area, I motioned to her to tread warily; no need to give the game away before we started. And I must say, you could have heard if not a pin certainly leaves falling and rabbits bolting and birds twittering. I climbed a tree. She occupied a stump about equidistant between the main sett and the outlier near where I'd seen the cubs disappear. Within strained-neck sight of each other! Half an hour later this was the sum total of our viewing, hardly the emotional conflagration we'd banked on. Into the bargain the gnats were eating her alive. It really was ridiculous. The gnats, I mean. They rendezvoused from miles around, drawn irresistibly by lust for their favourite juice coursing through her veins, driven mad at the prospect. Have you noticed how some special people have this charm? My blood is the stuff of which common transfusions are made. Theirs is the nectar of the gnat world.

My wife was never still, seeking relief. And not only from the gnats. She left her stump and rested her back on a tree, indifferent to camouflage or hiding, more concerned to find support than stay out of sight. Some badger-watcher!

Now what was the woman doing? Not merely swatting, but waving her arms like a windmill gone crazy. Might as well go home. I strained my neck again. Her agitation grew. She waved. Gesticulated. Pointed. *Pointed?* Behind me was a boar near an entrance I'd ignored, sniffing the evening air, sitting, standing, grooming – totally disregardful of her open presence! Within minutes he was joined by a sow and a cub, then a second cub, the new arrivals staying close together, apparently anxious to leave him to himself. Suddenly the sow bolted for the entrance, the cubs scampered after her, and finally the boar followed.

My wife was smiling, gratified at her first sighting, doubtless also smug at having pointed out the badgers to me.

Down the incline, running as though for its life, came a cub out of nowhere, its tiny legs clearly inadequate for the speed its fear demanded, and dived straight into the same entrance.

Again we settled, she still at the front of the tree, surely an ostentatious deterrent to every self-regarding badger thinking of emerging. Yet within minutes, her battle with the gnats unabated, out popped the biggest boar, simply magnificent, I'd ever set eyes on. As though to invite our admiration, he ambled to the top of an incline, sat panda-like, scratched under his armpits, groomed extensively and then did something unique in my experience of badger gymnastics. He lay on his back fully outstretched, and repeatedly rolled up to touch his toes, not unlike a heavy-weight champion in strict training. Up, down, up, down, stopping only briefly once to scratch his belly. Or was it to rub complaining muscles? Whatever the reason, my wife and I could barely contain our amusement. Then, still quite alone, not a sign of another badger or badger movement, utterly contemptuous of my wife's sustained hyperactivity against the gnats, he wandered off further up the incline, doubtless to begin feeding.

I wish I could report that this one night turned the gnats' dinner into a badger-watching fanatic. It didn't, to put it no stronger. For days the bites nearly drove her mad, landing her in a chemist's shop, pleading for any kind of relief. But at least she does more readily appreciate why I, distasteful to the gnats by comparison, take every oppor-tunity for watching badgers, their performances rarely repetitious – thought I wouldn't complain about that – and usually incorporating a variety of innovation.

7

And I only asked about the badgers!

One of the unlooked-for by-products of my badger-watching was the growing number of people I kept stumbling across, each a character, all united in their willingness to talk about their own badger experiences, the *second* best way for a novice like me to learn. The *best* way? Need you ask?

A man told me of a sett worth looking at beyond the church in the next village, first turning to the left along a rutted farm track, past a farmhouse, and keep going to where the track petered out.

'You can't miss it,' he said.

I took the turning, came to a car park, into a children's playground, followed a path by the river and reached a heavily barbed wire fence with a notice: *Keep Out. Private.*

'It must be,' my informant corrected himself next time we met, 'the *second* turning. You can't miss it!'

This time it did lead me past the farmhouse and proceeded, by the look of things, over the horizon. But before getting anywhere near that far, I came across two men talking, one at the wheel of a Land Rover with its engine running, the other half his age and twice as unfriendly.

'You realize,' he threatened, 'this track leads to nowhere!'

I mentioned badgers.

He smiled. The man in the Land Rover turned off the engine.

Plenty round here, they both said. And even before I could enquire about the reputed sett at the end of the farm track, the Land Rover driver was reminiscing about a boyhood experience with his dad. The trouble was, he recalled, one lamb after another was disappearing, and his dad brought up on a farm, farmer all his life, didn't doubt the culprit was a fox.

He searched everywhere for the earth, combed the farm and district, asked the help of local poachers who claimed to know every step of the area, but found nothing, not a sign of a fox. Yet still the lambs were being taken.

'I remember,' the man smiled, 'the morning Dad decided that if a fox wasn't to blame, it had to be a badger. Simply had to be. And the more he thought about it, the stronger became his certainty. I was only ten at the time, thirty years ago,' he chuckled, 'but the pair of us went to the sett, on the farm for years. And what do you think we found? The remains of eighteen lambs – *eighteen* – all of them, Dad said, taken by a rogue badger too old to feed normally.'

My eyes filled with scepticism. I knew badgers reputedly took the occasional lamb, as I've mentioned, but eighteen! By the same badger!

'There *are* rogue badgers,' he emphasized. 'Not many, but they can be awful mean, an absolute menace near a sheep farm. Once they get the taste of lamb there's no stopping 'em. It's either that or starve,' he concluded.

'Eighteen, you say?' My suspicion of leg-pulling requested confirmation.

'I saw for myself,' he said; 'nothing of "I know a man whose friend told his wife who told her mother . . .", you know the sort of thing! I was an eyewitness. Watched Dad dig out the badger. Nothing else he could do, in the circumstances. Of course, it wouldn't be allowed now. Need to get a licence and call in the RSPCA or the vet or somebody official to do the job. Not that Dad meant the badgers any harm; he didn't destroy the sett. We had 'em on the farm for as long as I can remember.'

The other man, initially unfriendly but now the opposite, said there was a sett on his farm, though he wasn't sure it was active at the moment. He'd show me if I liked!

'See that tree over there,' the Land Rover man pointed. 'If you walk in a straight line beyond it towards that water tower, you'll find any number of setts.' He revved the engine. 'Lovely creatures, badgers,' he said. And wishing me well in my search, he pulled away.

The other farmer and I set off along the track.

'Do you know who that was?' he asked.

I admitted my ignorance.

'He played rugby for Wales,' he intoned, not unlike a priest at some high altar, as though unworthy for such revelation to pass his lips. 'Played for Wales, he did; Cardiff Arms Park!' He paused, overcome, proud and humble at his close association with such incarnation. 'Do you,' he collected himself, 'ever go to the Royal Oak?'

'Strange you should ask,' I said, 'a farmer on the – '

He cut me short. 'He sometimes drops in there. Lots of farmers round here do, sort of unofficial club.' He laughed conspiratorially. 'Well, it's nice to talk to people of like mind!' Another pause. 'Played for Wales, he did . . .'

Nearing the end of the track, he led me into a field, up the side of the hedge, and pointed. There were three entrances, with tunnels apparently going under the track itself. The badgers' digging, he explained, could be a bit of a problem; they caused parts of the road to cave in. Otherwise he hardly knew the badgers were there at all. In fact, admitting he wasn't sure they were in residence at the moment, he asked what I thought.

On the near side of the track was thick undergrowth, with more undergrowth on the other side, and beyond a field of ripening wheat. I bid him farewell as I set about investigating, which in the event was less than straight-forward. For to get into the wheatfield involved walking quite a way down the track, climbing a chained gate, doubling back part of the way, going through another gate, then a field, and finally scaling a fence – the lot admittedly demanding little more than time. But both fields were saturated with recent downpours, the result being my trousers were quickly soaked up to my kneecaps as I pushed round the perimeters. Better to wait, I decided, for the sunshine and a drying wind. This apart, my original informant had underlined that the sett he had in mind was further on from where the track petered out, and I was clearly some distance from that point yet.

Some half a mile nearer the water tower, I came to a farmhouse ruin, sick at heart that such a building, surrounded by nothing but breathtaking scenery, was being allowed to fall down. Doubtless it would cost a fortune to renovate, but why this neglect in the first place?

The nearest farm buildings stood out on the horizon. Still following the track, I turned a corner, and was surprised to find what was clearly a permanently stationed caravan in the middle of nowhere, a perfect site for getting away from it all. A dog greeted me, making it unnecessary for me to knock; and through an open door a couple and their three children looked up from their game of cards to smile.

'Badgers!' they reacted. 'We haven't seen any, and we've been coming here,' the man calculated, 'for more than twenty years. Badgers,' he laughed. 'Not round here. Ask the farmer.' He pointed to the farm buildings. 'He's bound to know.'

The track continued right up to the farmyard, where a man was unloading his car outside the dairy.

'Sorry,' he said, 'I'm a stranger to these parts; only here to repair this milking machine.'

A car approached from the other side of the farmyard.

'Can I help you?' the driver called.

Now in case you're wondering, I can confirm that badgers do more than entertain with their ballet performances. The very name – badger – breaks down social barriers, overcomes shyness, and within seconds gets people talking like old friends. Actually, it also – as I was to discover shortly at the village pub – occasionally leads to a verbal punch-up, but more about that at the appropriate moment. On this occasion I was charmingly assured that badgers were definitely on the farm, though the farmer's wife, the car driver, confessed she herself had never seen one. Here or anywhere else!

I can't tell you how many times I've heard this same admission. From deep-dyed countrymen and country-women – never seen a badger in their life! They know quite a bit about badgers, will argue the pros and cons about whether these animals of the night are responsible for spreading bovine tuberculosis, and what should be done in consequence, will come up with reports about badgers taking lambs or hens or cats or what-have-you; yet they themselves, far more than I thought possible, sheepishly acknowledge they've never set eyes on a badger! Most odd. In fact, their lack of personal involvement with badgers is matched only by their almost total ignorance of insects; *too much* involvement there, of course, but not in terms of the identification of more than a handful of species.

Anyhow, the farmer's wife said her husband would know about badgers on the farm, but unfortunately he was out, working one of their other two farms. At this precise moment a dilapidated Land Rover passed the farmyard and disappeared round the back of a barn.

'That's my husband,' she said. 'He won't be far away.'

Maybe. But I couldn't find him. Not then. At the same farm, however, a few days later I first learned why the farmhouse ruin was being ignored. Repeated flooding had rotted the foundations, resulting in a condemned order being served; and a subsequent application to renovate or rebuild had been turned down. My informant shook his head, clearly despairing of all bureaucrats. About badgers he could hardly have been more decisive.

'None round here!' he said.

Yet the rugby international had been so confident, absolutely certain. Perhaps he'd meant the next farm, barely visible, but still – give or take a mile or so – in line with the water tower!

Eventually I reached an outbuilding, heard voices and found myself confronted by an attractive young woman who introduced herself as the farm secretary. I mentioned badgers. She disappeared into an inner office and soon returned with the farm manager's permission for me to look wherever I wished.

'You should,' she added, 'have a word with our cowman; he knows all about the badgers, sees them often as he gets the cows in for the morning milking. He's in the milk parlour at the moment. Come on, I'll show you.'

We found him, six cows being milked either side, standing in a well deep enough for his arms to be level with the udders, convenient, he explained, for him to plug the machines on to the teats. We watched as he washed the teats of a new row of six and started the whole operation for the umpteenth time.

'Badgers!' He laughed affectionately. 'Cheeky little blighters. They sometimes come right into the farmyard, early morning, just before dawn.' He plunged in another four

76

teats, calling over his shoulder that when he was a lad he had a pet badger; kept it under his bed; reared it on the bottle; nearly drove his mother mad.

Having settled another six cows, he stepped out of the well, looked me up and down like a chief inspector a criminal, and said he'd show me the setts if I liked, when he'd done milking, about six o'clock. I had to decline. What about ten-thirty in the morning? Again I had to decline. One-thirty in the afternoon? he persisted. And in walked another row of six, drilled to perfection, each cow knowing its order and place.

The farm secretary said she knew the locality of one sett on the farm. Would I like to see it now? So off we went in a Land Rover, she bubbling with what she called an excuse to get out of the office, I frankly incredulous at such helpfulness.

And what a sett! In the middle – almost the middle – of a large field growing grass for silage; eight entrances within a circumference of perhaps thirty strides, no more. The nearest tree was on the far boundary of the *next* field! Plenty of woodland beyond that distance, a perfect habitat for badgers. But what made me look even harder at this sett was the absence of worn paths; plenty of evidence, I thought, of badgers in residence, but barely the suggestion of comings and goings.

The explanation was forthcoming the next day, when I met the cowman as arranged.

First, though, badgers momentarily forgotten, he had to check a heifer soon to calve. We walked through the farmyard to an adjacent field containing half a dozen rams recovering from their tupping exertions, and about twenty expectant cows, one of them, I immediately saw, with a hoof poking from its vulva. The tail was raised like a distress signal, an impression reinforced by its owner's raucous mooing and heavy breathing.

'She's fine,' the cowman said.

We climbed into the Land Rover and drove to the sett of yesterday, which, he told me, the badgers used only as an outlier, staying for limited periods. This made sense to me, but raised another query. The grass, virtually ready for cutting, provided excellent cover. What happened when it was cut? If the badgers weren't in residence at the moment, presumably their use of the sett wasn't regulated by considerations of cover?

'We never cut too near the entrances,' the cowman said. 'The land's rutted, as you can see; difficult for the cutter to get close. But in any case we wouldn't want to give the badgers a hard time.'

Amazing!

Again in the Land Rover, we headed for the nearest woodland, climbed a fence, threaded our way through heavy undergrowth and came to a clearing – evidently, in the light of the nearby entrances, a play area for badgers. The cowman led me from one cluster of entrances to another; the wood was a perfect habitat for badger longevity. I chose my tree for watching, and promised myself an early return.

My expectation was that now we would drive back to the farmyard and part company. I'd seen two setts, and the cowman was surely concerned about his calving heifer, spasmodically mentioned in our conversation. In the event, we drove to a different part of the farm entirely, followed an ancient dirt road, left the Land Rover of necessity to continue on foot, and examined first one sett, then another and a third, before – the heifer increasingly in mind – he pointed to where I should keep looking for setts he himself didn't know about but didn't doubt existed.

As we drove back to the farmyard, it was hardly surprising that our talk should be of calving, and of what he called a year in the life of a cow. It starts, he said, as far as he is concerned, with the cow giving birth; two to three weeks later her coming on heat is due to commence; if it doesn't, another twenty-one days, and subsequently at three-weekly intervals, otherwise the vet! Sharpish. To get the cow pregnant again at the first possible moment is crucial. Hence the ready availability of a bull on permanent standby or the person from the Milk Marketing Board with AI. This farm, incidentally, invariably uses a bull of its own, unique in my experience.

A cow's gestation is nine months. About six weeks before the calf is due, she is dried off (no more milking) and given a complete rest, time to renew herself and prepare for the impending travail.

Then the annual cycle starts all over again.

'Have you,' he asked, 'heard a cow bulling? Broadcasting to the whole world she is ready for a bull?'

I nodded.

'In that case,' he smiled, 'you understand how we know she's in season.'

Still chatting, we ambled from the farmyard to the field with the heifer. He was apparently utterly unconcerned. I asked whether I should leave my dog behind. He thought it might be a good idea, for the dog's sake!

Soon I was to know what he meant.

Need I mention, the dog was making herself inconspicuous throughout what the cowman called his lunch hour – settled at my feet in the Land Rover, walking to heel, keeping her feet if not her scent away from the setts, with little prompting from me. But a heifer in labour was something else! Yes, better to keep the dog well away.

The cowman talked to that expectant mum as to a

frightened child: quietly, soothingly, reassuringly, all inter-laced with endearments suitable for wooing. The heifer mooed all the louder, early notice of her determination not to reciprocate. He kept talking, calming her down, driving her unhurriedly towards the open gate from which I'd cleared the rams.

Cleared them just in time! She careered through, round the back of a barn, along a concrete leadway ankle-deep in dung, to a complex of farm buildings, and – wooed all the time by this remarkable lover – finally agreed to do no more than lead us a merry dance. An adjacent stall in the labour ward was occupied by a cow and her dead calf, born the night before and awaiting collection by the knacker.

The cowman cogitated; he couldn't make up his mind whether the heifer was ready to deliver more than the solitary hoof peering from her vulva. Only one way to find out, he said, sticking his hand up the cow's vagina to his armpit and groping around – what he called 'loosening things up a bit', a comment too modest by half, judging by the next half minute. For he positively rocked that calf to and fro, up and down, all *inside* the cow; pushing and pulling with enough abandon to leave me exhausted. As for the cow, she appeared totally unconcerned. Certainly the mooing stopped; well, almost.

He climbed out of the cow, grabbed the immediately appearing pair of hoofs, and gently pulled. The calf's mouth came into view, revealing a tongue well and truly hanging out; and red.

'That's what I've been waiting for,' he said. 'The colour of the tongue; always goes red when the calf's ready to be born.'

He disappeared, and returned stripped to the waist, a precaution I too should have heeded. In his hand was what looked like a jug of washing-up liquid, no different from

80

the stuff we use every day even when not delivering a calf. The cowman lathered his arm, then the vulva, then thoroughly the hoofs and tongue peering from the backside; and gently pulled. In my anxiety to miss nothing, I stood too near the cow's arse. Once more, gently, ever so gently, he applied power. The vulva stretched, but nothing like enough. More washing-up liquid. And a rope from the hoofs to a hand machine that worked not unlike a car jack.

He pulled on the ratchet of this machine held against the cow's hind quarters. Another pull, still ever so gentle; no rush, no tearing of the vulva. More liquid. Another tug on the cow jack. The calf's nose was now well out. More liquid. The eyes, the upper face, slowly, slowly; then – *plop* – the whole head was out and visibly getting bigger!

More liquid. Another pull. And the calf slipped to the straw, the loveliest bloody mess I'd ever seen. Not wasting a second, the cowman grabbed the calf and pushed a piece of stiff straw up each nostril, desperate to make it cough or sneeze, to get it breathing. And I actually watched this newborn filling itself with life – like a living corpse returning from the brink.

A noise from the cow brought me back to earth. She was emptying herself of air or wind; nothing offensive, rather like a celebratory fart of unbelievable duration. Then came the afterbirth, spraying everywhere. As I say, in my anxiety to miss nothing I was standing rather too near, proved by my splattered hair, face, shirt, trousers, shoes – the lot.

The cowman laughed. 'You should have stripped off, like me!' he said.

I should.

The cow herself looked over her shoulder in wonderment, perhaps about her sudden feeling of emptiness, certainly not about the calf. She ignored it completely; not a flicker of interest or any attempt to lick it clean. The cowman, his eye on the clock for afternoon milking, led me out, the calf still in its birth bag.

'I'd rather have had a heifer calf,' he said, 'but this one's welcome enough. We'll sell him for meat in about eighteen months.'

He glanced over his shoulder at the newborn and the apparently indifferent mum.

'She'll soon be sniffing around the calf,' he laughed, 'and looking surprised to find her own smell. Lick him clean in no time, and the nutriments in what she takes off will be good for her.'

Having collected my dog, I followed the cowman's example at a tap of lukewarm water in a building next to the milking parlour. Understandably, he was in high spirits, glad to get behind him what he feared might be a difficult birth, but in the event one of the easiest, he insisted.

The pair of us thoroughly washed but still stinking like a cowpat, we walked next door to what I imagined would be my point of departure. In truth, I was already pushed for time.

'Would you like to see the milking?' he asked.

So the three of us set off to bring the herd of Friesians in from pasture, my dog – retired farm sheepdog, experienced with both sheep and cattle – walking to heel, for all the world as though she was back in business and delighted at the prospect. Barely out of the farmyard, the cows just about visible, the cowman began to call them, not in words, more like a jingle. Whatever, the cows stopped their grazing and set off in our direction, not all of them, not those furthest away and perhaps just out of earshot. He continued to call as we walked towards them, and now the stragglers began to get the message. Apparently reluctantly, until they saw the dog!

Soon the entire herd was heading for her. She looked expectantly at me. In my ex-townee fashion I assumed she was appealing for protection. I pointed to the gate. She interpreted this as a command to work, like the good old days! In a flash she was off, round the back of the most distant cows, not to escape them but to push them on.

They scattered, regrouped, put their heads down in her direction and charged. Not backing off at all, she went for the nearest, head on.

Pandemonium.

Half the trouble was, I didn't know how to work her. She kept looking to me, puzzled at the absence of commands, wanting to put these marauders in their place but not knowing how. My only concern was for her safety. Take it from me, Friesians, normally gentle as lambs, can be fearsomely uncooperative with a dog!

'You'd better put your dog on a lead,' the cowman laughed.

I didn't hang about. In no time the pair of us were hot-footing it to the gate, chased by ninety predators jostling like crazy to get to the dog – I think it was the dog! – first. Her reaction was to strain to get at them and put them firmly to order.

Soon *I* was running, concerned for the dog, you understand; chased by the horde, I was not a bit scared, merely terrified. As for the dog, this indignity was intolerable! She pulled and uncharacteristically barked, asking only the freedom to settle these brutes once and for all. Meanwhile, the cowman was in some sort of apoplexy of merriment.

Have you, by the way, ever considered, perhaps witnessed, the courage of a sheepdog? Its refusal to be intimidated, with all the odds stacked against it, never backing off by as much as a whisker? Takes a bit of believing, especially when the herd*ed* take it into their empty heads to become the herd*ers*. I have to confess I've seen a few sheepdogs put to flight, their nerve failing at that crucial moment of defiance by ram or cow, but these exceptions underline the rule. On this occasion, however, I myself prevented such a confrontation by tearing ahead of the herd, dragging the complaining dog with me and thereby fortuitously getting every cow in sight to precisely where we wanted them to be, in double-quick time. At least I had the presence of mind to head straight for the milking parlour.

By the time the cowman arrived, he could hardly speak for laughing. Nevertheless, undeterred by this display of my farming inexperience, he allowed the first dozen cows to take their places in the parlour, and handed me an apron! That moment of his trust and my disillusionment remains with me for something else entirely – the way clouds of flies left the cows at the entrance, routed by a magical deterrent; barely a fly was to be seen inside.

Sprinkle the teats, the cowman showed me, to soften them.

Operate the automatic feeders, each cow its own special ration according to the stage of its gestation.

Hose the udder, and particularly the teats, thoroughly.

Tear off six sheets from what looked like a kitchen roll, one for each cow, and wipe each teat dry.

Press a button at each stall to release a suspended milking machine, and another button to make the suction for plunging in the teats one by one.

I started with the sprinkling and graduated within thirty minutes or so to the plunging in.

Did *you* know that no four teats on a cow are ever identical? Come to that, not even two teats are identical; every single one is unique in shape, size and much else –

cuts, warts, softness, length, degree of co-operation for plunging in; one hard (suspicion of mastitis), one almost too modest to handle, hardly worthy of the name. Yet all three hundred and sixty of this Friesian herd's were functional, too many of them waiting to illustrate my notorious ham-fistedness.

Finally – my arms killing me, my back aching, my aspirations to be a cowman aborted – it was all done: two hundred gallons of creamy milk, top grade of course, ready for collection by tanker from the Milk Marketing Board.

And I only came to ask about the badgers!

Walking home, I couldn't help but wonder. Two milkings daily, four hundred gallons, and all by one man; one man filling his spare time with calving, observance of oestrous cycles, arranging the availability of bull or AI, feeding individual rations, regular inspections, knowing when to call the vet, keeping the milk parlour and all its equipment scrupulously clean, plus a thousand and one jobs inescapably associated with the entire herd, in this case 167 animals at various stages of development, with a hundred or more in milk.

Imagine – one man! Seventy-hour week, twelve consecutive days on, two off. How did he do it? With great difficulty, that's for sure, judging by my one session. But *why* did he do it, do it cheerfully, wanting nothing different, as long as his strength held out?

It's not a job, he'd told me, it's a way of life.

'You smell funny,' my wife greeted me.

I bathed and changed everything.

'You still smell funny,' she said.

No wonder the divorce rate among cowmen is reputed to be high, well above average.

8

Swimming badgers

Long before badgers seriously crossed my mind, I met a villager somewhat removed from the village itself, little realizing at the time that our chance conversation and the events that flowed from it, one triggering the next, would eventually lead to a significant development in my badger education.

Presumably Rosa had her share of disappointments, like the rest of us, but judging by outward appearances they made no difference. She gave the impression of total contentment with her lot as wife, mother and grandmother, a contentment she herself attributed not least to the cottage she and her husband had occupied for virtually the whole of their married life.

It was well off the beaten track, with just one other cottage nearby, and approached by a single narrow path of wild flowers in summer, a quagmire at the worst of winter. The only other building in sight was a tiny chapel, occasionally used for services from spring to early autumn, but throughout the year attracting hordes of ramblers and tourists anxious to acquaint themselves with its history and the magnificence of its craftsmanship.

At my first visit a black labrador was making irreverent use of a tombstone. It wagged a welcome, and soon – our relationship firmly established with pats and ear-kneading – we wandered together from one forgettable epitaph to another, each of them, as far as I could decipher the lettering, commemorating a villager long since forgotten;

and reassuringly illustrating to what extent our expectation of life has increased!

A child's voice called. The dog promptly disappeared. Screeches of laugher. And from the other side of the chapel a girl of five or six rushed into view, playfully chased by the dog. Not batting an eyelid at my unexpected presence, she invited me to join their game of ring-a-ring o' tombstones.

Another voice called. Urgent. Insistent. The child continued to play, not a care in the world. I followed the voice through the chapel door and found a woman on her knees, engaged in, she laughingly told me, her favourite form of devotions – dusting and polishing. Assured her granddaughter was up to no mischief in the graveyard, she resumed her devotions, paying particular attention, I could hardly fail to notice, to a stain on the altar carpet.

If only visitors would kindly remove their muddy boots at the door; she despaired of removing the mark completely.

'It's not so bad if they stay on the stone floor, but so many of them seem to think they'll miss something unless they walk all over the carpet. People!' Her merry face mocked exasperation. 'They're so *funny* – come in here, whisper reverently, and wipe their boots before leaving. You'd think, wouldn't you . . .' Her voice faded. 'Just listen to me,' she laughed at herself, 'you'll be thinking I'm a grumbler!'

The stain on the rich blue carpet was proving remarkably resistant. She stood up, moved across to a pile of cleaning materials and returned with a tin of something. Made doubly conscious of my own muddy boots, I instinctively backed away, anxious not to add to my offence.

'Oh, dear,' she sighed, 'you *do* think I'm a grumbler!'

And *she* seemed genuinely distressed, as though the stain was entirely her fault. To be honest, looking at it again, I wouldn't have been surprised if her initial justifiable indignation had turned nasty. As it was, she cheerfully gave the impression that anything less than a perfectly unmarked carpet would reflect upon the Almighty Himself.

Eventually it was done, and she began to pack up.

'Have you,' I enquired, 'been chapel cleaner for long?'

'Let me see,' she began to calculate, 'must be thirty-four years; that's right, thirty-four years, almost as long as we've been in the cottage. I'm better at polishing than praying,' she laughed, 'and every little helps!'

Her granddaughter was still skipping among the tombstones. She lingered, watching her, anxious not to spoil the fun.

'Pity children have to grown up in cities,' she remarked, 'packed like sardines, nowhere decent to play. Must be awful for them. Especially on those building estates. Our youngsters always had plenty of space – fields, woods, trees to climb, no traffic to worry about. And our neighbour was so good; he let them help with the milking, the lambing, collecting eggs, things children love; and now the grandchildren. Aren't we fortunate!'

I could only agree as, hand in hand, accompanied by the still irreverent labrador, Rosa and her youngest clone disappeared towards the cottage.

I lingered in the ancient graveyard, increasingly aware that the place throbbed with life not death – birds everywhere, a new grave ablaze with flowers, two magnificent yew trees almost as old as the chapel itself, and suddenly, from nowhere, a sheep and her lamb.

Now I can't imagine anyone, country-lover or not, not being charmed by a lamb at play. Infectious gaiety. This one bounded about, occasionally suckling, mainly indulging its celebration of life, undeterred by the ewe's near total preoccupation with this lush and for her exclusive pasture.

Until it spotted me!

Then it bolted to the protection of its mother, who – impatiently dismissing its attempts to suckle – continued to stuff herself. An ideal lawn mower. How clever of the archdeacon to think of it.

How long I sat there I've no real idea. The shadows of the tombstones began to lengthen, and imperceptibly, idly watching this solitary sheep cropping the grass, further charmed by the lamb, I felt profound contentment. Such calmness. And peace. Words not recalled for years struggled to surface:

> This other Eden, demi-paradise,
> This fortress built by Nature for herself . . .
> This blessed plot, this earth, this realm . . .

Reluctantly I stood to leave, prompted, I confess, by thoughts of a favourite pub. Two men approached the lych gate, both known to me as farm workers halfway or so between our village and the next. They strode among the tombstones, eyes darting, and disappeared to the other side of the chapel.

Moments later the ewe and lamb shot into view, chased by the men, both pairs equally determined to frustrate the other. This blessed plot suddenly became a funfair.

The men mumbled threats.

The ewe baaed defiance.

The lamb bleated. And bleated.

I wanted to help, but knew it would be injudicious to interfere. In the event, I watched the pursued and the pursuers charging among the tombstones, all four too frenetic to achieve other than pandemonium.

The real problem was, of course, that the men didn't have their dog with them. I could only surmise they were either facing an unexpected situation or viewed the use of a dog in such a setting as lacking in reverence. Whatever the explanation, they quickened their futility with the expertise of shepherds accustomed to working sheep with a dog. A good 'un, too, take it from me. And sheep can be awfully bloody-minded without a dog to keep order.

Another problem was the size of the hole in the fence through which the pair had broken from their rightful pasture next door. It looked altogether too small. Indeed, I wondered whether this explained why the other sheep with their lambs hadn't followed into the graveyard, for usually one leads and the rest quickly fall into line. On this occasion, the grass inevitably greener on the other side of their enclosure, they appeared inexplicably indifferent.

The younger shepherd lunged at the lamb, presumably reasoning that if *it* could be returned, the ewe would automatically follow, and for his trouble fell flat on his face, no nearer a solution. At the end of another five minutes of chasing, grabbing, cursing, and muttering contradictory endearments, the situation was unchanged, apart, that is, from growing evidence of both desecration and an abundance of free fertilizer among the tombstones.

Long ago, I recalled, a man also up against it was prepared to give his kingdom for a *horse*. These two, I didn't doubt, would gladly have settled for a sheepdog.

In the end, cornering the ewe by the larger yew tree and the fence, the older shepherd managed to grab a hock; and together they bundled the wanderer through the gap. Naturally the lamb followed, though only after tilting at the fence two or three times, searching for the way.

Then it was smiles all round. The men set about repairing the fence. I started to walk, another sort of refreshment in mind.

* * *

In the pub, talk was about the recent shearing champion-ship and Rosa junior (Rosa's youngest child and only daughter), unintentional collector of broken hearts. It wasn't, I should immediately emphasize, that Rosa played fast and loose or led her idolaters a merry dance. On the contrary, liking them all, each apparently no more than the rest, she answered their individual ardour with an impish not to say tantalizing unavailability. Even this doesn't quite give the right impression.

Rosa simply wasn't ready to settle down. In other words, she thought the lads of the village, one by one, wanted to be too serious. Her limit was nothing more than friendship. And if they couldn't accept her terms she treated them with what could easily have been mistaken for intolerance.

What made her so popular, easily the most sought-after young lady in the village – her stunning looks apart – was her sense of fun and the goodwill she generated almost everywhere. Almost! There was an exception – the home of the champion shearer on the marsh.

Despite his rippling muscles and manly appeal, Rosa treated him like the rest of her youthful admirers; but his proud parents interpreted her attitude as a personal affront to more than their son, proof positive she was too big for her shoes, a proper little madam.

The days leading up to the annual shearing championship were marked by gathering excitement, centred in our village on a lad brimful of his eighteen years, as strong as a heavy horse and fired by an ambition to beat the champion from the marsh, to beat him for a reason other than shearing. Need I mention he was among Rosa's devotees, hopeful that his triumph at the championship would pene-trate her emotional armour? And when I saw them together on a couple of occasions, on the second walking unhurriedly through my favourite wood, I assumed their common interest was becoming more than the speedy shearing of sheep.

The venue for the championship was Reedmace Farm, big enough to accommodate simultaneously sheepdog trials, a lamb competition, craft stalls, an exhibition of wool and weaving, and, of course, a bar and buffet. By late afternoon six shearers were left to do battle in the next day's final, among them our village hope and the champion from the marsh. To be frank, judging by the heats, he looked unbeatable, but we weren't entirely without hope, for our man seemed stronger, better able to sustain the physical effort demanded.

What bothered us all most was the champion's technique, particularly after we'd learned that winning wasn't simply a matter of shearing faster than anybody else. The judges also took into consideration the quality of the shearing itself, keeping a watchful eye on the degree to which the sheep were free of snicks and cuts.

The modified cattle shed was packed as the finalists, stripped to the waist, their bodies already glowing with perspiration, walked to their positions. Each stood in front of a pen containing his sheep. And as they were individually introduced, the din was deafening, terrifying the sheep even beyond their already excessive liveliness.

An official started to count down, ten, nine . . . three, two, one, BEGIN! Each competitor grabbed and upended a sheep in one lightning movement, pinned it between his legs and set the shears humming. In little less than a minute the first fleece was off, all in one piece, cast aside to be wrapped by an assistant, and another sheep grabbed.

Slightly ahead was the man from the marsh.

The crowd was going crazy. Support for our man turned us into a mindless mob screaming encouragement, pleading for superhuman effort. I wouldn't have believed it! The frenzy. The pandemonium. The assumption that noise was synonymous with encouragement.

After five sheep, the champion from the marsh was still ahead and going like the clappers. Our man was just about equal second, with two or three others. At halfway these positions were barely altered, though the lead was definitely shrinking.

In all the hubbub no one, I tell you, was more carried away than Rosa. This usually self-possessed beauty was beside herself, shouting the name of her hero as though less than his triumph would mark the end of her world. I began to watch her almost as much as the shearing.

But hang on a moment! What was Rosa shouting? Surely not. Yet there it was again – the name of the man from the marsh!

And when, a few days later, I noticed the engagement ring she was wearing, I was compelled to acknowledge that our village hope, strong as a heavy horse or not, had been pipped at the post in more than shearing.

Anyhow, it was that coming together of Rosa and the champion which led to my discovery that badgers are consistent in nothing more than their inconsistency, certainly when it comes to choice of habitat. You see, he told Rosa about badgers on the marsh; and Rosa told her mother; and her mother, knowing of my interest, told me; and I, knowing the marsh was flat and open, told myself it took a bit of believing.

Badgers go for cover – trees, bracken, woodland, all of them conspicuous by their absence on the marsh.

Badgers (I thought) disliked water, never hard to find on the marsh.

Badgers prefer to dig in chalk and sand, light soils, easily shiftable, hardly handy on the marsh.

It was, however, the bleak openness of the place that persuaded me that the champion might be a wonderful shearer of sheep, but he knew nothing about badgers. Stood to reason.

Yet Rosa senior kept telling me that her daughter's fiancé kept telling her that badgers were on the marsh in number. With all the wisdom of a novice expert, I ignored the claim, my authority reinforced by what I read. Alas, Rosa senior must have been less than delicate in communicating my disbelief. Back came a message naming a farm bang in the middle of the marsh where badgers reputedly had recently been seen. Only one response was possible in the circumstances.

I knocked on the farmhouse door.

Now farmers on the marsh, as you can imagine, are primarily sheep men, even if some also grow cereals. Their first love is never in doubt. This man who answered my knock was a case in point – driven to give more of his land to the plough but thinking of himself as fundamentally a sheep farmer; like his dad and his dad's dad and dads back for generations before them. Sheep men. On the marsh. The two belonged to each other, justly world-famous.

But badgers? He hadn't seen any himself, though his brother-in-law, who had more time for that sort of thing, reckoned he'd spotted one beyond the dyke some weeks back.

'Would it be all right if I took a look?' I shared his scepticism.

'Feel free,' he said. 'Any time you like.'

'Would *now* be convenient?'

'I'll come with you,' he said, 'and show you exactly where I mean; make sure you don't get yourself lost.'

We climbed a gate rather than untied it, crossed a field, jumped a ditch, and he pointed – at a couple of holes.

'Looks like an earth,' I said. 'I'm not sure, but I think so.'

'Foxes!' he smiled. 'Wouldn't be surprised. Plenty round here. See 'em often. They don't bother me, not all that much. Mind you, they can be buggers at lambing.'

He left me to it, the pair of us still not sure. Earth? Or sett? I couldn't make up my mind. Earth, I thought; yet remembrance of the sighted badger wouldn't stop nagging. That brother-in-law wasn't likely to be mistaken; he'd lived on the land all his life, by all accounts something of a naturalist. None the less, the more I looked, the less uncertain I became. The holes were too tall and narrow for badgers. Definitely an earth. Might even be a warren entrance, though admittedly it did maintain its size as deep inside as I could see; unusual for a rabbit.

Ah, well, I silently pontificated, just as I thought. Rosa's champion might be marvellous with sheep. As for badgers . . .

I strolled beyond the dyke; in truth, I later discovered, on to a neighbouring farm, much of it under the plough. The field in which I found myself was especially large, clearly the result of hedges ripped out and fences removed. The latter were sparse for another reason – artificial waterways, one of them wide enough to involve me in a giant detour. Fortunately it was a lovely day – a nip in the air, sun up, temperature rising fast – an invitation to keep walking.

In the distance I spotted a mechanical dredger at work, made for it, and asked its operator about badgers. He was too polite to verbalize the look in his eyes.

'Badgers!' he chortled. 'In this wilderness? I've heard

they're on the marsh, but never seen any myself. Mind you, I don't live in these parts; never here at nights. But badgers here . . .!'

I was left in no doubt what he thought.

I turned for home, crossed a bridge to avoid a waterway further down I'd already found difficult to leap, followed a ditch full of water draining away to an outlet near the bridge, and settled for a badgerless withdrawal. No point in searching any more, not more than casually.

I knew all along there weren't badgers on the marsh.

Even as I write, the shock of suddenly being stabbed wide awake by the evidence of my own eyes grabs me again. I stopped in my tracks like walking into a brick wall. And stared unbelievingly. It couldn't be!

For a start, the constantly draining water at the bottom of the trench was deep. Second, there was absolutely no cover, not even a tree within a hundred and fifty strides. Third, on either side of the trench the land was ploughed, stretching forever, giving an impression of flat emptiness.

Yet unmistakably there was a badger sett. A real beauty. Eleven entrances, half a dozen at least clearly in current use. *And* – the sign that drew my attention in the first place, never mind the arguments about how or why it was there – a ball of hay. Old bedding out to air? New bedding surplus to requirements or waiting to be taken below? Either way, it was so indisputably the work of badgers.

And yet . . . I thought badgers didn't like water! These entrances were within an arm's reach of this constant draining, almost guaranteeing at least wet feet on coming or going. Little did I realize at the time that badgers could swim, didn't care tuppence about living near water, even presumably sometimes preferring it, this lot anyway. I simply stood staring, trying to reconcile the undeniable with the unbelievable. For this was definitely an active sett in the – theoretically! – unlikeliest habitat possible. It didn't make sense.

I went home and wrote to an acknowledged authority. What about this, I asked, a sett with no cover, exposed to the steppes of the marsh, with water lapping at every entrance?

He must have chuckled to himself as he replied that the badger, like Nature generally, is nothing if not at times unpredictable. *Un*natural.

'You'll learn,' he said.

I did!

9
Seeing red

I'd picked up from somewhere – setts near waterways or not – that badgers don't like rain; they prefer to stay below, snug and dry, rather than risk a soaking. It made sense, at least superficially. Plenty of other hairy creatures, some as tough as nails, like, for instance, working sheepdogs, detest heavy downpours; but I still found it hard to believe that a badger's hunger wouldn't take precedence over its wish for comfort, always supposing, of course, that rain was a deterrent in the first place. Animals generally, domestic and wild, are governed by nothing more than their stomachs. It was hard to accept that badgers, whatever the circumstances, would be an exception.

It had been raining all night, all day, and was still pouring as I drove to the sett, parked in a lay-by, and made my way through the woods, which somehow seemed less than friendly, indeed almost threatening in these conditions. Yet the premature dimness in no way reflected my spirit.

Ask any badger-watcher, and he or she will confirm that waiting expectantly at a sett, no matter how many times repeated, never loses its excitement. On this occasion, despite gusting wind adding to my discomfort by showering me from every leaf on my tree, I was content to be a fool. Especially when a badger ambled across my viewing area, from where I'd no idea, shook itself like a dog after a bath, and made for what I knew was a feeding place. True, it didn't hang about; no scratching or the usual antics immediately after emergence. But if one badger was prepared to brave the elements, there might be others.

And, of course, this proved to be the case. One after another, *alone*, at intervals of minutes – unique in my experience at the time – each made a beeline in the direction of the first. What also intrigued me was that they didn't emerge from any of the entrances under surveillance, some six or seven unfailingly used before. In fact, it was my concentration on these that almost caused me to miss a slight movement in the corner of my eye; I imagine I would have missed it altogether but for the colouring. Red. More than sandy. The coat of a red setter!

I panicked. I almost jumped from the tree to chase it away. A dog at a badger sett! The consequences could be horrendous, not least for the dog. Only days before I'd read an eyewitness account of a badger being attacked by three dogs – an Alsatian and two terriers – and the trio had been seen off after a blood bath; one of them died within minutes, the others required urgent attention from a vet. But instead of jumping I took a long hard look. And nearly *fell* out of the tree.

A badger.
Definitely red.
Absolutely no question.
Impossible?

Back home I told my incredulous wife; and reached for the badger bible, turned to the index, the word *red* – nothing, then to *colour*, and there it was, authoritative confirmation that I hadn't been seeing things, rain or no rain:

The true erythristic form has a distinctive gingery appearance on back and sides, while the normally black underparts are a sandy red. The colour appears to be due to a different form of melanin in the guard hairs. The density of the pigment and its degree of reddishness varies slightly from one animal to another. There is little doubt about the colour of their eyes. The majority appear to be light brown, but some with reddish eyes have been described.*

A *red* badger! Admittedly it remains my only sighting, and I now realize that such badgers aren't all that rare; but I'll tell you this – in my limited badger-watching circles I know quite a few individuals who'd give anything for such a glimpse!

Let's call it beginner's luck. And all because I turned out in a downpour! Don't tell me badgers dislike rain more than they love their stomachs.

I've had only one other unusual sighting, unusual, that is, for me. It was at the same sett. I'd been there two nights before and seen fourteen badgers, though I think at least four of these were duplications (badgers returning underground and emerging again), and wanted to explore the area to which this lot had made tracks, presumably to feed.

It was shortly after two o'clock in the afternoon, meaning my dog inevitably was with me. We weren't attempting to be particularly quiet; not bashing about, obviously, simply concerned to follow a clearly defined badger path from entrances to play area to part of the wood with denser undergrowth. We reached a sort of ridge still some distance from the top of the incline. I noticed a spaghetti junction of paths; my dog indulged her nose to the point of inebriation.

Suddenly she took off. I called her back, urgently. Ten strides or so away was a badger! Two things, probably related, were immediately self-evident. The badger was extremely slow in picking up not only our scent but our presence at all, remarkable considering the noise we were making; and, second, even when alerted, its departure was

* *The Natural History of Badgers* by Ernest Neal (Croom Helm, 1986, p. 27)

belaboured. The reason, as far as I could see, wasn't injury or the like, simply old age; this ancient sow, on her last legs, her coat mangy, was too weary or worn to get away with customary badger alacrity.

Badgers sometimes live to a ripe old age, up to twenty years or so, though the evidence for such longevity applies only to one in captivity. Precisely how long they survive in the wild is an open question. An average of two to three years is thought likely, with an age range of from soon after birth to twelve or so years.

Apart from the dead badger I came across by the roadside in our badgerless village, the only other corpse I'd found was of a cub at a sett beyond the next village, a cub too small to be above ground! There seems little doubt that most badgers die naturally in their own beds. Knowing the end is near, they remain below or crawl to their sleeping chamber, which is sealed off by members of the sett immediately after death. This explains why skeletal bones can sometimes be seen near entrances, the result of old chambers being reclaimed by a new generation of badgers.

I have in front of me now a sow's skull discovered in such circumstances, lying alongside evidence of fresh diggings, an ancient sow, judging by the extent to which the molars are worn. Weeks later at the same sett, I thought I'd found confirmation that badgers sometimes bury their dead above ground. Judge for yourself. A couple of days before, I'd come across what looked like a partly eaten corpse, clearly a badger, attracting a lot of frenzied activity from bluebottles buzzing above the putrefaction and finally settling deep inside to lay their eggs. I'd returned expecting to find a heaving mass of maggots bloating themselves. Instead, the corpse had gone, presumably buried beneath fresh earth covering the area.

My assumption was, of course, that this was the work of someone on the farm, concerned to keep the stock free of infection; but extensive enquiries indicated otherwise. The farmer was adamant neither he nor his men had been near the place for days. In fact, they hadn't even known about the dead badger.

So how come the burial?

There is an eyewitness account of a badger funeral by the naturalist Brian Vesey-Fitzgerald.* He tells of a sow facing upwind, standing with head lowered, her back rippling in a most agitated manner, uttering what he describes as a very tiny subdued snuffle. She was also jerking her tail from side to side which made her look 'very ridiculous'. Then suddenly she raised her head heavenward and made a weird cry, half whimper, half howl, eerie enough to make the hairs on the nape of the neck of this vastly experienced nature-watcher stiffen.

The sow moved briskly to a disused rabbit warren nearby, and soon it became apparent that she was digging in the warren, punctuated by an occasional grunt. Eventually she came into the open again, disappeared down an entrance at her own sett, and almost immediately reappeared, sniffing the air and behaving in a most agitated manner, once coming to within a stride of the observer's hiding place yet taking not the slightest notice of him. By now he was convinced he was to witness something unusual.

Again the sow went to the warren, giving the impression 'there must be something there she wanted and could not get out, so anxious did she seem'. Every ten minutes or so she returned to her own sett, disappeared, and emerged sniffing the breeze in an anxious manner. This behaviour

* *A Country Chronicle*, by Brian Vesey-Fitzgerald, (Chapman and Hall, 1945, pp. 125–33)

continued for almost a further two hours, until another badger suddenly came into view 'round the bluff'. At first it skirted the bushes, but as it came nearer, the naturalist could see that it was not, as he'd first thought, the dominant boar he knew well but an apparent stranger. The sow stood stock still, her back ruffling agitatedly and her nose touching the ground. The newcomer advanced to within a few strides before halting, his nose also lowered.

Now commenced, Mr Vesey-Fitzgerald recorded, an extraordinary scene. First the female, with a jerky upward toss of the head and a swift downward movement until the nose touched the ground, uttered a thin, musical, whistling sound, rather as though the wind had been sharply expelled through the nostrils. The sound lasted – perhaps it was more a squeak than a sound – just as long as it took the head to complete the motion. At the same time she moved forward with two tiny jerky steps, the hairs of her back ruffling very quickly. The moment she stopped, with her nose almost touching the ground, the male, standing exactly opposite her, went through the same procedure.

The performance over, both badgers moved to the sett and disappeared, the female leading with the male following nose to tail. They were gone for some time, causing the observer to wonder 'in the nasty manner of human beings, whether the domestic life of the badger was quite blameless, and when this Don Juan of badgers would go, or if he would be caught by an irate husband, and what would happen if he was – in fact my mind was behaving in a thoroughly civilized way – when the visitor reappeared, or at least his tail'.

As gradually the whole of him came into view, it was clear he was dragging something – the body of a badger. Had he, the naturalist queried, added murder to his other sins? But no sooner was the body clear of the entrance than the female appeared. Together they dragged the body to the rabbit warren; the male had hold of the corpse by a hind leg; the female's contribution was less self-evident though beyond question.

At the warren the observer 'could not really see what they were doing. It was not hard to guess, however, and soon the indistinct sounds of scratching confirmed my guesses. Father was being buried!' Shortly they were finished. There was no further performance of any kind, no sounds, no noise at all, no more touching, nothing. The male, moving quickly, vanished the way he had come. The female returned to the sett, looked straight at the naturalist, and disappeared below.

Mr Vesey-Fitzgerald concluded: 'I went over to examine the warren. Earth had been shovelled into the mouth, and packed by the bodies pressed against it. It would have been easy to loosen the earth and exhume the body inside, but I did not. That would, to me at least, have been sacrilege. I turned away and, after examining the track, clearly defined, from sett to warren, tramped off home, thrilled and hungry.'

To say that I'm not entirely convinced in no way questions Mr Vesey-Fitzgerald's powers of observation or integrity, both beyond dispute. It's just that other badger men and women of vast experience say they've never seen anything of the kind. I'll keep an open mind, and – like Ernest Neal himself – go on hoping that one day I too might witness such an event.

First-hand experience is obviously preferable to hearsay, even if the hearsay comes from impeccable sources! I am, for instance, now able to make my own contribution to the debate about badger bedding – completely renewed, or brought up periodically from the sleeping chamber for airing? Perhaps a bit of both?

The occasion could hardly have started less promisingly. A cub sniffed at the entrance I was watching, then half emerged; and a horsefly alerted me to its company by sinking its fangs into the back of my hand. The vehemence of my reaction prompted the cub to withdraw below! That, I thought, was the end of my badger-watching for the night.

Horseflies! I often wonder why they were invented at all. The species I have particularly in mind are named cleg. Dull grey, they lack the common decency to indicate their presence until it's too late; silently home in on exposed skin; there's nothing at all to warn their victim, precluding any sort of evasive action. Doubtless you too know how their noiseless feasting guarantees discomfort for days.

I hesitate to attribute their existence wholly to an omnipotent sadist whose jokes are always in bad taste, hesitate because of my initial attitude to wasps. They, too, as far as I was concerned, were totally without justification, especially when I'd seen the results of their frenzy after being disturbed by a cutter during haymaking. They'd chased the tractor driver from the field and most of the way home, turning his face into a sting cushion, bloating it within minutes, and warranting a 999 call. It took a bit of believing, I can tell you, that wasps had a creative side to their nature and were in fact fundamentally on the tractor driver's side in his fight against pests ruining his crops.

In any case, badgers love wasps – bees too! – and eat a whole nest of them at a time, with the relish of children with honey or ice cream and strawberries. No problem with the stings. They merely rise their impenetrable hair, leaving only the snout to worry about – the reason why they never attack a wasps' nest at the entrance, but always straight down, to the heart of the business. In this way they wreak havoc before the inhabitants realize what's happening. And badgers *do* enjoy the grubs plus, of course, the wasps themselves, stings and all – in itself an excellent reason, you might think, for the existence of wasps.

But the horsefly? Probably it too has its redeeming features, though they escape me at the moment. The nearest I know to one was suggested by Jonathan Swift, in his observation on the flea:

> So, naturalists observe, a flea
> Hath smaller fleas that on him prey;
> And these have smaller fleas to bite 'em,
> And so proceed *ad infinitum*.

The interrelatedness of the natural world; every species exploiting another, and all for the benefit of Man! The arrogance! Anyhow, even if the horsefly feeds upon other pests, and in turn is itself fed upon, this in no way justified its aptitude for being literally a bloody nuisance at my expense as I prepared to welcome the other half of the emerging badger.

Happily, within a couple of minutes of my squashing retaliation, a black and white face reappeared, sniffed as though not needing reassurance, and led out a quartet of cubs, the lot barely able to contain themselves before playfully going for each other. I say *playfully*, though at times the squeaking and squealing protests about bitten ears and tails sounded too urgent for fun. Maybe this was why they didn't hang about: a few rounds of snarling followed by murderous lunges, and they were away, presumably to search for food.

Next from the same entrance came two sows, initially suspicious, then sedate, apparently surprised at the absence of the cubs. I'd assumed that the quartet belonged to the one sow, but perhaps – as sometimes happens – more than one family were playing together. These two sows, in any case, made off quickly in the same direction as the other five, and were soon lost to my sight.

Any more? I wondered.

As though to answer my impatience, a boar and a sow sniffed from the entrance, clambered up the mound, sat, scratched, stretched and briefly indulged in mutual grooming before ambling after the others. Ten minutes or so passed; not a badger in sight, and not likely to be, I thought. There had been nine already – I'd hardly reason to complain – but on show for only an aggregate of no more than five or six minutes.

Yet if the badgers weren't feasting my eyes, they were increasingly puzzling my ears. The noise from the direction in which they'd disappeared was surely badgers. Nothing, however, like I'd heard before; certainly not digging or snuffling or playful wrestling. Altogether different. Coming nearer and nearer.

I waited expectantly, straining my neck from my perch, trying to look round corners, trees and the undergrowth to my left.

Another boar – recognizable not only by its size but also by its flatter head and nose, plus the dome shape between its ears – waddled from the entrance, for all the world as though customary sniffing to check security was a waste of time, an exercise for the faint-hearted. Within seconds he was out of sight, apparently off to join the others.

The noise persisted, still nearer. Then a scut appeared, followed urgently by a bottom and a body and a black and white head frequently glancing over its shoulder. A boar. Alongside was a sow, prancing around, not lifting a paw or claw to help; watching not working.

Between the boar's forelegs was a ball of straw, big

enough to cause problems of manoeuvrability, but not too big to hinder speedy progress – backwards to the entrance. He guided it to the waiting sow below, who wasted no time in dragging it underground. Meanwhile the boar was already out of sight along the same path to start the whole operation again – as I eventually again heard and witnessed. And then once more – three times in all before darkness made further easy viewing impossible. But judging by the amount of bedding I saw taken below, each time by the sow, after the boar delivered it to the entrance, there couldn't have been much room for old bedding too. Or could it have been that growing cubs were now demanding larger sleeping quarters, and extra bedding to go with it?

That's the trouble, you see. A watcher of limited experience can never be absolutely sure.

10
Digging ain't baiting!

Watching Bess at work – something I loved to do at every opportunity – it was hard to believe the sheepdog was once nothing more than an unwanted stray. She had pitched up at the farmhouse door, and refused to go away – refused, take it from me, despite every encouragement from both the farmer and his tender-hearted wife.

'Bloody mongrel,' he said.

'Poor thing,' murmured his wife.

'Don't feed it,' he warned. 'You'll only encourage it.'

So she fed it. Stealthily.

What sealed the stray's unconditional acceptance was the day she rounded up a herd of rampaging bullocks, herded them without as much as a by your leave, fearlessly drove them from farmyard to pasture like a veteran, which perhaps she was.

'She's a good 'un,' the farmer told his wife, who smiled, nodded, patted the dog, and said they might as well keep her!

Which is how she came to be committed to the expert care of Elijah, a wise old shepherd who'd worked on the farm for years.

He was the kind of man you don't often meet, and certainly can't forget in a hurry. Soft white hair, piercing eyes, and horny hands of strong gentleness, doubtless the outcome of his long years of delivering lambs. Equally unforgettable, unnerving at first acquaintance, was his habit of never using two words where one or less would do. That, too, was probably the result of his shepherding, the long hours alone with his sheep, his only companion Bess, the former stray.

A silent man. A man of old-world charm. The first time he raised his hand to forelock in greeting I was embarrassed, until I realized he did precisely the same to pretty well everybody, not as a mark of social inferiority, but out of a deeply ingrained courtesy, almost a reverence for life. I more than respected him. His wholly unexpected death was like a blow from a poleaxe.

Obviously, then, if I was so affected, how in the world must his widow have felt? She and Elijah had appeared so devoted, mutually dependent. She once told me that she and her husband *communed* with each other, told me laughing nervously, half afraid, I think, I wouldn't understand. In fact, having watched them together, her meaning was crystal clear. Of course, you might well share my own initial scepticism – cynicism! – that their sparse words to each other were only too typical of ageing marriage. I merely repeat: they communed as naturally as their love was unostentatious and delightful to behold.

She took his death in her stride. Barely appeared to mourn, certainly not in conventional ways. Whereas we in the village had expected her to fall apart, she seemed almost radiant, comforting rather than seeking comfort. I waited for the rebound. It never came. Perhaps, after all, my unworthy scepticism hadn't been so far off the mark! Indeed, Bess appeared more urgently in need of consideration. She refused to work. She took to her former ways of disappearing, often just when she was needed to work the bullocks – her speciality – and generally gave eloquent notice that the farm without Elijah wasn't worth the trouble, exasperated, screaming, threatening farmer or not.

And where did Bess go? Unerringly, persistently, to Elijah's cottage, naturally. With equal determination, the widow shooed her away and told her to get back to the farmhouse where she belonged. Under no circumstances, the farmer instructed, was the widow to feed the dog or allow the delinquent to settle by the Rayburn. She was needed on the farm. Elijah or no Elijah – and the farmer grieved like the rest of us – the work must go on, doubtless the point Elijah himself would have made.

Everybody agreed, apart from Bess! And in the end, a compromise was reached. Bess could live at the cottage on condition she was available for work as required. Imperceptibly, over a period of perhaps three months, no longer, she became the centre of the widow's world. Don't misunderstand. It wasn't that Bess remotely replaced Elijah, but the new partnership increasingly resembled the old, notably in terms of mutual dependence and unspoken affection.

They walked miles together, over the downs and through woodland beloved by Elijah, scene of his first shy confession of love, his widow told me, something of a trysting place now, she said, to which she and Bess frequently returned.

Dozing in her kitchen one afternoon, she heard neither a knock, the door opening, nor footsteps. Opening her eyes she found herself staring into the face of a total stranger. Gypsy? Tinker? Vagrant? She wasn't immediately sure. Her heart thumped. She tried to cry out, but no sound came.

'Don't look so worried,' the voice muttered. 'I've only come to ask if you have anything to sell – antiques and the like. *Anything*. For cash, of course.'

The widow glanced round for Bess.

'Your dog's playing outside,' the man laughed. 'Having the time of its life, by the look of things.'

'I don't have anything,' she muttered. 'Nothing, nothing at all. And you have no right to walk in like this . . .'

'I'm going.' He quickly turned to the door, calling over his shoulder, 'Sorry I gave you a fright.'

And was gone.

Like Bess.

From that day to this she's been missing. Vanished into thin air. Not a trace. Despite wide-ranging efforts to find her.

The farmer doesn't doubt she was stolen – spirited away by the unwelcome visitor and quickly sold, for what purpose the widow dare not imagine. The only thing she's sure about is that Bess is being kept away against their joint wishes.

The little cottage seems empty. Its solitary occupant continues to feel distraught. Choked with grief. Drained of strength, even the will to go on. I met her again recently, some weeks after the dog's disappearance. She was weepy, and feeling awfully guilty – at seeming more upset about Bess than Elijah!

'I wasn't,' she protested. 'How could I be! But what must people think?'

At which moment – remembering some of the innocent banter I'd overheard in the village pub – I knew beyond question that Elijah was absolutely right. Why use two words where one or less would do!

Talk in the village pub, needless to say, isn't always so innocently hurtful or coloured by the latest gossip. We do have our more serious moments. I mean, who could rest comfortable abed, with holes in the road outside the village shop getting no smaller despite murmurings and more to the county council; complaints about noise from the village hall – complaints, to boot, from a newcomer who had moved into the house nearest this centre of carousing. From jumble sale to flower show to the over-sixties annual tea and entertainment to barn dance in aid of our rebuilding fund, he had belatedly discovered that country peace and quiet cannot be guaranteed, day or night, even the wrong side of midnight!

Village-pump politics of such immensity are bound to bring sobriety into the best of village pubs, specially when the post office, part of the village shop, is again threatened with closure, unknown dogs are savaging sheep and lambs yet again, another bus is removed from our already decimated time-table, and – a real life-and-death issue – badger-baiting is on the increase.

What complicated this otherwise surely clear-cut matter was a young terrier man with a justifiable reputation for fair play. Everybody hereabouts knows he isn't above a spot of poaching – or, more usually, hunting with permission – gun or snare at the ready with equal expertise, but woe betide any of his like-minded buddies who treat the intended quarry with less than respect. Admittedly he draws the line at crows, which he can't abide, and he isn't over-partial to magpies, but his fiercest detestation is reserved for anybody within his own sporting circle who isn't, as he puts it, *responsible*! He condemns them out of hand, and not only behind their back, calling them louts and worse if women aren't present. One of his main concerns is that they are to blame for the bad name suffered by *sportsmen* like himself who strenuously avoid unnecessary suffering of their prey, the very opposite of the rabble: depraved sadists, who care for nothing but their own vicious enjoyment.

What focused the matter again was my reference to growing signs of badger-baiting on the other side of the county, prompting the badger group to which I belong

113

issuing an appeal for volunteers to sustain a round-the-clock vigil. Some of the older villagers and – I couldn't fail to notice – a number of recent arrivals among us found it hard to believe that badger-baiting still took place at all. Wasn't it now outlawed, the badger a protected species?

So I mentioned the experiences of a Kent woman at setts she constantly patrols and where, incredibly, the badgers, having musked her, accept her as a member of their social group. Not only has she been threatened but also physically assaulted by badger-baiters caught in the act, on a number of occasions.

Nor was this restricted to one or two local areas. I'd recently received news of badger-baiting in another part of the country: of 437 known setts, 13 per cent were undisturbed, 18 per cent indicated regular persecution, and as many as 25 per cent were now extinct through diggers and baiters. No doubt at all, this was a general problem, and not only restricted to Britain. Dr Jim Barry, Scientific Adviser for the Irish RSPCA, had expressed desperate concern about, would you believe, the Munster Badger Baiting Championship!

Such contests were run, he claimed, on semi-military lines and extremely hard to detect. But due to the vigilance of one of the society's rangers, the championship was finally tracked down, held on the day of the All-Ireland Hurling Final, when almost every spare Garda had been drafted to Dublin to control the enormous crowds! The local area had been left in charge of a sergeant who, single-handed, was unable to make arrests with such huge crowds present, and had to be content with recognizing individuals and recording car numbers. Regretfully, the badgers involved had been spirited away.

We know, Dr Barry concluded, that the All-Ireland Badger-Baiting final was held in November.

It was, in fact, this latter reference that brought the young digger forcibly into the discussion, adding, as I've intimated, unwelcome complications, for he was definitely on my side, rather like the devil condemning sin. And there was no doubting his sincerity. What he didn't say about those badger-baiters wasn't worth a mention. He'd shoot the lot, on one of his more compassionate days! As far as he was concerned, there was all the difference in the world between responsible diggers, like himself, and badger-baiters, who deserved everything that was surely coming to them, sooner or later.

'Digging ain't baiting,' he kept repeating.

And this bestirred an old regular at the bar to reminisce about his dad and the once traditional Boxing Day badger dig attended by virtually every man and lad in the village.

'Great times, they were,' he said. 'Plenty of beer – a barrel or two – Christmas cheer aplenty, ferreting for the young 'uns, rabbits galore, an occasional pheasant by mistake.' His eyes twinkled. 'And occasionally a badger. In them days,' he concluded, 'we knew the difference between digging and baiting!'

'That's right.' My main antagonist welcomed this unexpected corroboration. Digging, far from harming the badgers, actually helped, he maintained, as weedy or diseased animals were humanely put down, concentrated numbers dispersed to less populated areas, and problems related to farms and the like solved without unnecessary suffering. 'You bloody do-gooders' – he sounded the opposite of offensive – 'are a menace, not least to the poor old badger.'

Superficially this all appeared reasonable enough, though I knew digging in practice was something else; but what really got my goat was his claim, without so much as a blush, that badgers were neither afraid of dogs nor entirely unhappy to have their formidable fighting capabilities put to the test!

Badgers, he was emphatic, weren't fearful of dogs, terriers or any other breed. With *their* claws and teeth, they were able to take good care of themselves.

Not afraid of dogs! Harried and hounded front and rear, no means of escape from murderous jaws, jaws presumably unfamiliar with the reputedly humane attitude of the diggers waiting to close in! Badgers, I knew, were brave; but courage didn't mean the absence of fear.

'Are you suggesting,' I asked, 'that a badger welcomes, even enjoys, the challenge of a dig? That trapped underground, maybe for hours, and finally hustled into sack or cage, eventually to be put down as weedy or diseased, or released into a totally strange, less populous territory, it nevertheless remains grateful for the chance to prove its courage, the opportunity to tear flesh and muscles of dogs and diggers alike in the process of itself being torn apart? And what about the unashamed baiter, intent on deliberately incapacitating the badger – broken forelegs, hind legs chained, claws pulled, jaw restricted, eyes blinded – before pitching it into the maelstrom of fit and fighting dogs?'

'Digging ain't baiting,' he repeated. 'Haven't you heard,' he asked, 'about TB in cows? Infected by badgers! So what happened to control the disease after digging was outlawed? Tens of thousands of badgers, diseased or not, were put down if their sett was too near an outbreak. Bloody stupid it was,' he said.

I readily agreed. Between August 1975 and June 1982 cyanide was pumped into 4,000 setts, each condemned for being within a kilometre radius of an infected herd. And this period included a year during which gassing was stopped to enable experts at the Ministry of Agriculture, Fisheries and Food to think again whether it was really necessary! They subsequently decided to continue the wholesale slaughter, then changed their minds, but not before also discovering that the gas they used was inhumane, killing slowly and with agony.

In any case, why doom the badger in this way, as though it alone spread the disease? Foxes, moles, rats, weasels, never mind other species, were also possible carriers, so why not – to be strictly logical – exterminate the lot?

Infuriatingly the young digger interpreted all this as support for his case!

'Leave the badger,' he reiterated, 'to the responsible sportsman, in the same way the fox is left to hunter and hounds, pheasant and grouse to gunsman and retrievers.'

The discussion quickened and warmed, exposing raw nerves on either side, evoking unusual frankness, revealing surprising allies both ways. What became increasingly clear was the digger's and his supporters' attitude to wildlife generally. They passionately believed that such animals were theirs for the taking, provided for nothing more than *their* pleasure in any way *they* chose. I didn't question or doubt their hatred of cruelty or their sincere wish to keep it to a minimum – though ideas about what this meant in practice varied considerably – but I couldn't stomach their assumption that neither the quarry's unavoidable suffering nor the badger protector's opposition should be allowed to interfere with their enjoyment.

Doubtless the topic will crop up again!

Most pub talk is somewhat less contentious! A few days later, still exploring the wider area, my wife and I were walking for a full day by the canal, fascinated by its history, intrigued by its variation of locks, its fishermen, its boats, including at one point canoes from an activity holiday centre, and its magnificent setting incorporating one village after another, through sheep pasture and occasionally adjacent woodland, when – on the outskirts of the next village – we spotted a rose garden. Breathtaking. And not only because of the roses!

Some of the blooms were wearing hats, not unlike coolie hats. Apart from detracting from the loveliness of the total effect, it didn't make sense, not to us. We both stood gawping. Roses with hats!

Into the garden strolled an old lady, her face wreathed in smiles, obviously accustomed to such lingerers. We asked the inevitable question. Now she really laughed, as much, I imagine, at our incredulity as her own delight in talking about the roses.

'They regulate growth,' she explained. 'We take our best blooms to shows; and the secret of success is to match the rose at its peak perfection with the date of the judging. Very important, these hats; they shield the beauties from sun and rain – too much of either could be fatal. Mustn't bring 'em on too soon, you understand.'

We understood more comprehensively still a few minutes later, enjoying a ploughman's lunch. The man behind the bar casually mentioned that potential exhibitors weren't above a spot of sabotage – mucking about with other exhibitors' hats! I found it hard to believe. Not rose-growers!

11

Dogs, cricket – and badgers

Something else I was learning, too, unrelated to badgers: in a village like ours, ubiquitous dogs make a mighty contribution to human happiness.

And sadness!

Only the other day a woman was telling me how she and her husband went visiting friends some seventy miles away. Just before time to return home their dog went missing; there one moment, gone the next. And the most exhaustive and finally tearful search proved futile.

What to do? To leave their faithful sheepdog was unthinkable. Yet they needed to get home, her husband gently insisted, for his work in the morning.

Next day, beside herself with grief, she heard scratching at the door – and *there* was one exceedingly bedraggled and footsore dog! 'How,' she laughed as she told me, 'how did he find the way? Seventy miles! It takes a bit of believing, doesn't it?' Her eyes danced with pride.

Such happy endings are, unfortunately, no more manufactured than guaranteed. For instance, a retired lorry driver, a relative newcomer to the country after a near lifetime of living in London, made a point of taking his beloved labrador to the canal every day. He was gratified by her relish as she plunged in, seemingly indifferent to a drop in temperature or anything else. She simply loved her daily splash around.

Until, that is, she one day flung herself in, swam to the middle – and disappeared. Her owner watched unbelievingly, waiting for the dog to surface, not understanding why she was taking so long . . . too long; and even after five minutes he still couldn't take it in or accept it. His inseparable companion! Drowned! She loved the water, was as much at home in it as in the garden or tearing about the village green or roaming country lanes with him or accompanying his wife to the post office to draw their pension.

The vet, denied a corpse, could only conjecture. Probably a heart attack, he concluded, all over in no time, she wouldn't have felt a thing. But the retired lorry driver goes on grieving, poking fun at himself for being so sentimental – a trait he despises – consoled in part by the lovable replacement. Mark you, when I last saw them it was hard to believe he was still even remotely missing his first love. The dog, another labrador, was joyfully taking *her* first love for a walk, self-evidently where he didn't altogether want to go, and the resultant merriment at the mix-up suggested that the awful gap in his life was not so unfillable after all. In the end, he sank to a seat on the village green, slipped her collar and let her wear herself out with the other kids at play.

Ironically, what stands out about that occasion was another man who shyly sidled up to us as we watched our dogs sniffing and chasing each other. A most perceptive man, he said he preferred the sheepdog (mine) to the labrador, hurriedly explaining he used to have a sheepdog himself. And two cats, though, since last night, only one. Consequently sick at heart, he clearly needed to talk; and we two total strangers were presumably as good as any! If nothing else, we had time.

He explained that a stray from nowhere hung about the house, discouraged by him, fed by his wife; it simply wouldn't go away, despite all the encouragement of which he was capable – including a call to the RSPCA. What eventually clinched the stray's unreserved acceptance was the reaction of the resident cat, their only pet for years, who was normally aggressive to all feline outsiders. To the stray, virtually from the start he was the embodiment of affection. They shared the same sleeping mat and – more surprisingly still – the same feeding bowl, a double container ideal for the pair to eat side by side, with never a suggestion of one stealing from the other!

This stranger, his hair silver, his body healthily slim, came from a place I didn't know. He was crazy about village cricket – the main joy of his retirement. He said his wife came to love the ex-stray – no more than the other cat, of course, not officially, not even consciously; but he couldn't fail to notice how much pleasure she received from the newcomer, the tender nature of their relationship. So when his wife died a couple of years ago, he wasn't the only one who felt bereft.

'You know how it is,' he murmured, 'how people and pets become part of each other's life!'

The point was, he found himself sort of . . ., he struggled for words or with embarrassment, sort of drawn himself to the former stray; for his wife's sake – if you see what I mean, he appealed. And somehow this comforted him, the cat's association with his wife, the pleasure it had given her. Having the cat with him, he said, brought his wife nearer, closer. Could we understand?

Our silence spoke for us both.

'Last night,' he went on, 'the vet had to put the cat to sleep. She'd been poorly for some time, something to do with her kidneys, but I thought she was going to be all right. Then a couple of days ago . . . funny, isn't it?' He wrestled with his feelings. 'How an unwanted cat can worm its way into your heart!'

* * *

121

There are, I suppose, cats and cats. I've never been a cat man myself, finding them altogether too condescending and pompous, too arrogantly independent, but I concede they can be fun. Certainly that was my impression as I watched a litter of month-old kittens at Shepherd's Retreat, an isolated cottage at which I called frequently to talk with Harry Gregg and his wife about badgers, but also donkeys and Fred the goose and the history of our village going back to Harry's boyhood and beyond through his ancestors, farm workers for generations.

Harry was proud to tell me of a relative from America who recently spent six weeks searching all the church and chapel registers in our district for the surname Gregg.

'Just imagine' – Harry was awestruck – 'my forbears working this land, tramping these lanes, laughing and weeping, living and dying, all that time, from 1573! I wonder,' his eyes twinkled, 'if any of them played cricket for the village?'

The question, I quickly gathered, was much more than an afterthought, for cricket, next to his wife, was manifestly the love of his life. Not, mark you, county games or test matches, nothing so tame. Essentially *village* cricket, specifically the annual pitched battles between our village and the next but one. I should explain, our immediate neighbours didn't possess a team. Come to think of it, they didn't possess much at all, apart, that is, from an obsession about winning the county competition for the best-kept village, an aim reflecting their picturesque death-before-life approach to most things.

By contrast, the village beyond hummed with activity. At the last count they boasted some thirty-five clubs and societies, from a baby-sitting rota to bellringers to football to rambling to badminton to young farmers . . . on and on. Significantly, pride of place remained with their cricket team, whose do-or-die aim season by season was to prove their superiority over our equally dedicated eleven.

I say *eleven* though honestly compels me to acknowledge we possess a sort of playing twelfth man in the form of Alf Wagstone, our permanent umpire.

'You must have noticed,' Harry chortled as he eulogized Alf's prowess at the crease, 'the ever-present fag; the blinding puff of smoke from the corner of his mouth as the visiting bowler brings over his arm!'

Harry laughed at my scepticism – my lingering city naïvety? – and set about proving his point. Did I know about the time Alf was rolling a fag during an over, and the shooting stick on which he supported his ample frame at the crease was shot from under him by a ball going like a rocket? He went down rolling his fag, sat on the ground still rolling it, and continued to roll it as solicitous hands heaved him to his feet, the picture of a chain-smoker in crisis. His rasping cough too was a trial; most of all, according to Harry, when the other side was batting.

Not that Alf was always less than fair. There was an unforgettable moment when an aircraft suddenly appeared over housetops near the green as the bowler reached his point of delivery, quickly followed by a loud appeal. Alf brought his eyes down from the plane and pointed upwards to indicate he couldn't possible adjudicate.

The opening bat started to walk. Alf called him back and tried to explain. But the proud player wouldn't be patronized. He understood an umpire's raised finger! Alf was furious – the batsman played for us.

According to Harry, the only other time his umpiring authority was challenged was when a team from a brewery, reputedly in a cricketing class above us, condescended to grace the village green. Despite the game barely avoiding disastrous consequences as a ball crashed across our main –

our only! – road, nearly decapitating a passing motorcyclist, the real drama started a few overs later. The visiting batsman responsible for this mighty hit was bowled, one bail dislodged. He refused to budge. Alf raised his finger of dismissal. The man glared. Alf pointed to the dislodged bail. The man insisted both bails had to be off. Alf explained only one. The man repeated two. Alf walked up the wicket. Removed his fag. Told the man to go. The captain in the pavilion, a brewery executive, was called. Only then, still certain he was being wronged, did the batsman give way.

Appropriately, it was during this game that a prize long on offer was finally claimed. The landlord of one of our village pubs, fervent supporter of the cricket team for personal as well as business reasons, moved on retirement into a house overlooking the village green, undeterred by the constant possibility of a ball crashing through his front bedroom windows. Indeed, astonishingly he offered a bottle of whisky to the first batsman to fulfil the threat. Unfortunately he occupied his final resting place in the village churchyard before the fatal ball was delivered.

The batsman responsible called to apologize and incidentally mentioned the bottle of whisky! Not batting an eyelid, the new occupant immediately went to what passes for the village off-licence, and returned with the biggest bottle available. Very big. Only much later did she learn that the originator of the promise, affectionately remembered for his practical jokes, had planned ceremoniously to present a bottle of minuscule proportions.

Harry was now in full flight, one cricketing story following another, many of them centred upon a family whose name was a byword in our village and far beyond, outcome of generations of intermarriage. I was cautioned: as a comparative newcomer I'd need to watch my Ps and Qs in case unknowingly I found myself addressing a representative of this family labyrinth, most of all if cricket was being discussed. For *both* teams in the annual blood-letting between our village and the next but one included members of the family, whose loyalty to each other otherwise was absolute. Harry himself wasn't able to cast much light on their fierce cricketing prejudices. Superficially none of it made sense. Individuals living in our village turned out for the traditional enemy – brother against brother, son-in-law against father-in-law, bowler against batsman of the same lineage. Apart from cricket, our village was united – within reason, of course – but once within sound of ball on bat, ancient lines of partisanship were quietly asserted, no quarter asked or given. Generation after generation.

My wife and I first innocently brushed against this rivalry through the purchase of a raffle ticket. Oozing goodwill to man and beast, we settled comfortably on the village green awaiting the emergence of the umpires. Moving among the spectators were two men carrying a bottle of sherry, the prize on offer. My wife stuffed our ticket in her bag. The cricket started. Marvellous.

A snick. An appeal. And the umpire with a fag raised his finger. The visitors were 0 for 1. By tea the score had rattled on to 89 for 1, or something of the kind, largely because of the remaining opening bat. Once more the raffle-ticket sellers approached us. Would we, unbiased newcomers, mind shaking the tickets in a hat and picking out the winning ticket? My wife shook the hat, and I handed over the ticket. Our own!

We protested we couldn't keep the prize. We tried to pick another ticket or at least donate the sherry for next week's prize. They wouldn't hear of it. We'd won fair and square. Listening to this friendly altercation, a man from the next village but one cheerily suggested our cricket team couldn't organize a Sunday school outing, let alone a raffle. The only thing that took the smile off his face was the sudden collapse of the visitors – to 101 for 7, within the first four overs after tea. All out for 120-odd.

However, being a charitable man, I draw a veil over what happened when our worthies batted, or rather lined up at the crease, one sacrificial offering after another. Mind you, the light deteriorated badly, and heavy clouds caused the ball to swing wildly. Unpredictably. Unplayably. But I mustn't make excuses. We lost, as fairly and squarely as we won the raffle.

Our most memorable game of all, still a talking point at every opportunity or none, was the one that brought our village doctor, a relative newcomer, notoriety and, incidentally, instantaneous acceptance. Strangely enough, it didn't involve our arch-enemy from the next village but one. If only it had! We won the toss and elected to bat. By tea we were all out, leaving the visitors a winning target of just 92. And they didn't hang about. Even before our two pace bowlers had exhausted themselves, the score had reached 27 without loss.

Then the doctor, bleep conscientiously in his shirt pocket, came on with his leg breaks, a usual first bowling change that normally yielded less than necessary. In his first couple of overs three (or was it four?) wickets fell. By the end of his fourth the score was 30-odd for 5, with the batsmen continuing to grope like inexperienced lovers. Another wicket; and another; soon 8 down for little more than 50. All over bar the shouting, or so we thought. Their number nine and ten batsmen kept beavering away, mostly singles, an occasional boundary, every run resented, deplored. But they kept the score moving . . . 90 for 8.

Talk about excitement!

126

The doctor started another over, delivered the first five balls without conceding a run, and sauntered back to his mark. Why the delay? Why was he conferring with an umpire and leaving the field? The fieldsmen appeared not to know. They consulted the umpire. Only then, as they and both umpires hummed and hawed, were we spectators able to interpret the wild gesticulations.

The bleep had sounded!

Not even waiting to bowl the last ball of the over, the village doctor was on his way to the nearest phone. And this prompt response to duty both flummoxed the umpires and confounded our captain regarding who was to complete the over. One loose ball, he, his teammates and all of us agonized, could spell disaster.

Manfully if reluctantly, the captain himself prepared to go down fighting. He measured his run, altered the field placings, again swung his bowler's arm to loosen it, and was as ready as he was ever going to be.

A voice bellowed from the boundary. The doctor was seen waving his arms and running like a man chased by a Friesian bull, shouting unintelligibly but with sufficient volume to halt the half-hearted bowler. The bleep, it transpired, had sounded not so much a false as a less than urgent alarm. The patient could wait without danger!

Taking the ball, the village medico did his customary hop, skip and jump to the wicket, brought over his arm – and the score was 90 for 9.

In came their number eleven. His partner at the other end, perceiving this was no time for the faint-hearted, took one almighty swipe at the next ball, and heard his stumps collapse.

Perhaps our most famous victory.

To what extent the bleep interlude was responsible for

the batsmen's loss of concentration – their own vehement claim – remains a talking point to this day.

Little wonder Harry and I were never lost for words; he reminisced about cricket, I swapped my latest sett discovery. Unknown to almost our entire badgerless village, our neighbourhood was teeming with the lovely creatures.

As an example, I set out early one morning to check the sett virtually I alone knew about; across fields through at times avenues of mushrooms, more than I'd seen for years. The sett itself looked undisturbed and active – recent excavations, plenty of paw prints, dung pits overflowing.

Reassured, still feeling smug about my secret shared with only a select group, I made my way to another part of the woods in search of the maker of palings and the like, for me something of a weekly pilgrimage. His tarpaulin, like the old craftsman himself, was nowhere to be seen. Most unusual.

I followed the ancient track to a cottage he normally passed on his way to work, a place at which I knew he frequently stopped for a chat at the end of his day, mid-afternoon. A woman working in the garden told me he had been in the woods yesterday, collecting his things to transfer to another wood on the far side of the next village. He and I had talked about this at our last meeting, but I hadn't realized the move was to be so soon.

We continued, the gardener and I, to chat, mostly about foxes, the pair of us sufficiently newcomers to the country to exchange stories with the confident assumption of mutual interest. I mentioned an earth in the woods behind her cottage, the one I once suspected might be a sett. She knew it well; she and her husband had made the surrounds muddy, hoping to get a clear paw mark for identification, to compare it with a fox's and a badger's in their nature book.

'I suppose we shouldn't have done it.' She suddenly sounded self-conscious. 'In any case, it didn't work . . .'

But did I know, she asked, her eyes sparkling, about the badger sett in the private wood up the road? She hadn't seen the badgers herself, but the owner of the wood was sure they were there!

I pushed the bell of a large house opposite the wood, and found myself confronted – no other word will do – by a mixture of caution and gathering enthusiasm. Finally convinced I meant the badgers no harm, the woman who answered told me the details. Her handyman, a country-man to his finger tips, repairing and reinforcing fencing round the wood, was certain about the badgers. Further-more, she herself had come across a dead cub. No, she hadn't actually seen the badgers, but felt protective towards them; she worried about the local hunt and like-minded vandals. Recently one of her cats had been torn to pieces by the hunt.

'We've taken out an injunction,' she said, 'and made clear if they come on our place again . . .'

Would she mind if I took a look at the sett?

Not at all. Any time I liked. So long as on each and every occasion I rang the doorbell to warn them I was on my way. 'We can't be too careful,' she concluded.

There was no doubt about the sett; half a dozen entrances. But was it active? No sign of recent digging. Nothing to suggest bedding being aired or renewed, despite an abundance of newly cut straw nearby. I searched for a tree with claw marks. Nothing. And a collection of dung pits. Again nothing. Even so, the sett was unmistakable. Only one way to find out for sure.

An hour before dusk I was in my chosen tree, having pressed the doorbell en route. First surprise was a hare sitting on its haunches, looking like a small kangaroo, its size taking me by surprise. And when, presumably sensing my presence, it bolted, its sheer bulk again astonished me.

A fox slipped out of an earth to my right, not far from the entrances I was watching, and sat leisurely surveying the freshly cut field. I was tempted to suck on the back of my hand, simulating the squeak or squeal of an injured rabbit – an easy meal for a fox – bringing the predator nearer to investigate, but on this occasion my total silence was imperative. It wandered off eventually to start the night's hunting, still unaware, I think, of my presence.

Further to my right I heard a disturbance. Perhaps a badger digging? If so, I was in the wrong place to see, halfway up a tree overlooking what I thought was the main entrance. Not a sight of a badger for as long as I waited, well after dark. But if there was a dead cub, admittedly some time ago, and the fence repairer, experienced country-man, was sure the badgers remained, the fault was all mine. Clearly my next step was to have words with the man working on the fences.

12
A village wedding

I met Joanna through Paul, and Paul himself through his interest in badgers. They were both all of seventeen. His next-door neighbour heard in the village pub of my near fixation and mentioned it to Paul, who came knocking on our door. Would I take him to see?

Now I should make clear that Paul is no ordinary village lad. He is a seasoned countryman before his time, vastly experienced and knowledgeable, largely the result of his dad running a flock of eighty or so breeding ewes in his spare time – that's right, *spare* time; he's an electrician – and depending upon his only son's help. Paul knows all about dipping and dagging (arse trimming) and dousing (preventive medication) and hoof clipping and lambing and fitting elastic bands to wither lambs' tails and testicles, to mention no more. He is similarly knowledgeable beyond his years about ferrets and rabbiting, foxes and pheasants, yet *not* about badgers – not at the time he came knocking.

I didn't hesitate, for here was a lad at the crossroads, as ripe to become a so-called responsible digger as a badger-protector. I wanted him on my side. We finalized arrangements for the following Saturday night.

'You won't mind,' he appealed, 'if I bring Joanna?'

As we made our way to the woods, I reiterated my major concern. Badgers were unpredictable. Some nights they emerged long before dusk; other nights not at all. There was no guarantee we'd see anything. It was no use. They barely listened. Not only were *they* unconvinced by my earnestness, but *I* felt increasingly wretched at the possibility of this special vigil proving fruitless. The pair of them were so excited – blissfully confident – Joanna, particularly, bubbling at the prospect of actually watching badgers for the very first time. What added to the appeal for her was, I think, the knowledge that neither of her parents, brought up in the country, their forbears rooted in the soil of this neighbourhood for generations, had ever seen a badger!

We settled in my usual tree, I a little higher to make room for them side by side at a point offering perfect viewing. It was still quite light, my hope being, of course, that the badgers would co-operate early; but all too soon the gathering gloom gave way to darkness, finally almost impenetrable. Giggles below suggested this non-spectacular had become a farce. I sweated with desperation. Time to withdraw in ignominy.

I started to descend and whispered my intentions. Paul mumbled something and pointed. I switched on my brand-new red filter torch, outcome of my wife's persistence that I should have something better than the bicycle rear light I normally used; a light, she said, not only powerful enough to illuminate the sett surrounds, but with easy attachments to fix to wrist or button, plus a simple means of changing the beam from red to normal or green for other uses – like finding my way out of the woods!

Two badgers immediately gazed into the beam, their eyes shining like diamonds. They appeared unsure at first, then ignored it completely and indulged in their customary routine – shuffling, scratching, baiting each other, stretching, one with its front paws up a tree.

There are experienced watchers who say that badgers are indifferent in such circumstances because they think the light is either the sun, the moon or flashes of lightning – things to which they're naturally accustomed – and are therefore devoid of alarm. Whatever the explanation, this pair seemed to behave as if the spotlight made no difference. And not only the one pair, for two more badgers emerged, then another, five in all, each apparently revelling in the footlights. Never mind the red glow, the show must go on!

My one doubt about their total absence of fear or suspicion was, I have to confess, their reluctance to move far from the entrance, unique in my experience at the time. Normally they played around for up to fifteen minutes before moving off to feed, and not infrequently the time for play and grooming was much less, a matter of a minute or two. On this occasion they remained for thirty, and would, I imagine, have been happy to stay longer – but for *our* need to get home. I clicked with my tongue, they shot underground, and we quietly withdrew, the youngsters uncharacteristically silenced by the magic of it all.

No need to worry about this budding countryman or his girlfriend being on the side of the badgers.

I was gratified for another reason too. The five badgers had engaged in a whole range of noises, some new to me. There was what sounded like grunting, immediately flashing my mind back to the manner in which I'd warned off the farmer and his wife – possibly you remember! – who'd innocently seemed likely to mess up my watching in their wood before it was underway. Little had I realized then that badgers themselves actually grunted, or something very much like it, doubtless the reason why my noisy appeal to the farmer and his wife to clear off had done nothing to discourage the badgers' emergence.

Most common of the noises was a sort of high-pitched chatter, usually associated with cubs at play, but on this occasion mixed with a variety of growls and snorts, some suggestive of anything but mutual enjoyment.

Badgers also communicate with scents and postures. I've watched a boar musk a sow, sitting on her willing prostrate body. In like manner – plus sometimes the placing of dung pits – territorial boundaries are indicated, a warning to outsiders. Within these parameters might be a number of setts, each normally used by a distinctive social group, with the members free to come and go (visiting and possibly staying for a time at another sett). But woe betide the unwelcome stranger, certain to be challenged, maybe attacked, even killed if persistent, though I gather this is rare. Certainly all the badgers I've watched have been the opposite of aggressive in their relationships, give or take a few bitten ears and scuts among the cubs.

I'm still trying to work out at first hand the constitution of these social groups. The one I know best consists of two boars, three sows and, at the moment, four cubs now almost yearlings. How precisely they sort themselves out – two or three family groups? – I'm not sure. No doubting the dominant boar or the sows, though whether he fathered all the cubs, I again don't know. And something else continues to puzzle me. On one unforgettable occasion the number of badgers at this sett increased to fifteen, fourteen visible at the same time. I watched the lot gallivanting for ages, naturally charmed, not a little incredulous. Was it something to do with the mating season or nothing more than a social gathering of members from two or three setts within the territory? How can one be sure? I've never seen anything like so many together there since.

Setts have been known to consist of sows exclusively, with a boar or boars welcomed only for mating! But sows generally seek isolation for cubbing, each either dismissing the boar or boars from the sett and commandeering part of it for herself as maternity ward and nursery, or herself departing to an outlier, where she will remain throughout the suckling, taking care to keep the boar at bay. Otherwise he might cannibalize the lot, even his own.

Again I wonder why. Maybe he resents the sow's preoccupation, her single-minded devotion to other than his own whims and wishes. And the mystery thickens for me as I watch the cubs, well on the way to maturity, playing with the boar. Admittedly he isn't averse to clipping them behind the ears if they get too bothersome, but his uninhibited participation in the obvious fun and games seems far beyond mere tolerance. Why his change of attitude?

I puzzle, too, about what happens to the yearlings. Theoretically, in the fullness of time, they wander off to set up home on their own, either within the territory or to join a boar from another; but despite diligent searching I've never been able to trace this development. Surely they don't travel all that far. Or perhaps they do, at least some, Nature's way of avoiding inbreeding. I confess this was the explanation I once accepted, until being informed by Larry, the erstwhile mole-catcher, that incestuous relationships among badgers were not uncommon – boar mating with daughter, brother with sister, mother with son.

As I get to know my yearlings better, I hope to discover what happens to them once they move out. Do they simply wander off in confidence of a welcome elsewhere, or have previous explorations indicated their destination? As for the young boars, dangerously vulnerable outside their own territory, I can appreciate their reluctance to venture forth. Yet some undoubtedly have to move on. The weak? Or the strong?

There's clearly a lot of watching called for, with such

questions adding to the interest and excitement of each occasion.

Reputedly young men like Paul see visions while old men merely dream dreams. What makes one eighty-year-old human landmark in the neighbourhood somewhat different is that his dreams usually belong to the future. Talking with him, you could be forgiven for concluding he expects to live forever.

I initially met him in circumstances that typified the man. New to the district, I was trying to find my way across country to a village famous in these parts for its beautiful setting. The signs to indicate a public right of way petered out, and soon I was hopelessly lost. A distant farmhouse beckoned as a possible source of information; and this eventually confirmed my appalling sense of direction. The village I sought was miles away.

Having at last found it, I wandered in the general direction of home, still not without hope of finding the public right of way through woodland and pasture. Alas, it was nowhere to be seen, condemning me to a long way round on what passes in our neck of the woods for a busy road.

Working in a field was Methuselah himself, every movement clearly a painful struggle with his back; he bent with caution, and unwound in even slower motion. Did *he* know, I asked, of a public right of way? He didn't. Emphatically. Furthermore, having lived in the area for more years than he cared to remember, he knew there wasn't a public right of way, not over his land. Never had been.

Together we lifted the gate and hurdles he was erecting, the pair of us frequently pausing for breath. They would act as a filter for his sheep into a transporter, due on the morrow to take them for use at sheepdog trials. In between times he was remarkably ready to talk about himself, perhaps triggered by my dog, now retired, you recall, after working sheep most of her life. Was she, he wanted to know, a divide and wool and waistcoat dog? My blank reaction added to his merriment.

'It's the way a shepherd gets rid of a useless dog,' he explained. 'Before buying it, the possible purchaser naturally wants to see it working the sheep. So the shepherd tells the dog to *divide* them. It makes a direct approach, straight through the middle of the flock. In the process it bites a few backsides, just to show who's boss, removing wool by the mouthful, wool to make a waistcoat!'

Methuselah's eyes twinkled. 'The man with money in his pocket for a bargain is impressed. Bloody fool! What he doesn't know is that the dog isn't capable of a nice oval approach to push the sheep on gently, no need to nip or bite. It *always* goes straight through the middle, scattering and taking one mouthful after another from their backsides. A proper divide and wool and waistcoat dog.

'Is your dog one of them?' he asked, his back racked by the pain of his laughter.

By now we were chatting like old pals. He told me of how he bought his first farm, in 1942, for £6,500 – 150 acres and a farmhouse. Older and less wise heads in the village shook in disbelief. £6,500! For that! He must be mad.

'I reckon it's worth £200,000 by now, at least,' the old man chuckled in self-congratulation.

His other farm, where he himself lived, was obtained for £16,000, in 1964; and again the elders of the village assured him he'd been done to fork out so much for a mere fifty acres and a farmhouse, albeit with seven bedrooms, plus outbuildings in the farmyard.

'What do you think it's worth now?' He clearly thought

the question answered itself, underlining his business acumen.

A flock of some seventy sheep grazed or sat, contented with an abundance of nourishing sweetness.

'I work the lot myself,' he nodded in their direction.

I was, to be frank, a little sceptical. Lifting the gate and fixing the hurdles had proved beyond him single-handed. Apart from his years, he was also in constant pain, the result of a hip operation less than successful though still beneficial. His body creaked almost as audibly as his groans at the slightest bend. Sheer purgatory. So what about dipping and dagging and hoof clipping and dousing, not to mention lambing?

He read my thoughts, and roared with laughter. His farming neighbours, he explained, used his dip; they could hardly object to pushing his sheep through when they came with their own! As for the lambing, his daughter-in-law, whose husband wasn't interested in farming, was better than any vet.

'If she can't sort out the problem, difficult birth or whatever,' he said, 'we might as well cut the ewe's throat.'

'Does your wife help?' I inadvertently put my foot in it.

He paused, his eyes clouded, his lip trembled – the picture of a man undone.

'Twenty-four years ago to the day,' he murmured, 'we laid her to rest. In yon cemetery,' he pointed to a tiny Methodist chapel.

The gate and hurdles were by now securely in place. He moved unsteadily towards his car, pausing to glance over his shoulder.

'That public right of way,' he said. 'If you walk across the field to that oak tree, you'll find a hunt gate . . .'

I found it, and was immediately confronted by a puzzle, not of which way to go – this was self evident – but of why a marquee deep in woodland? There it was, alongside a smaller tent, but not a soul in sight.

Even Larry was baffled. A marquee in the woods! He promised to make enquiries. But first – and this was the main reason for his call at our cottage – would I like to go catching moles with him?

'I thought you'd stopped killing not only moles but pretty well everything,' I said.

'It's the wedding.' He intimated I was slow on the uptake.

'The wedding?' I asked.

We met near his favourite village pub, and made our way to the nobs' end of the village, gardens neat and tidy, lawns immaculate, apart from the one Larry had in mind. Normally it was, like the others, as smooth as a snooker table; at the moment, he said, it was more like a battlefield. Molehills everywhere. Enough even in normal circumstances to make the usually placid man who lived in the splendid house apoplectic; and these were anything but normal circumstances. In a matter of weeks the daughter of the house was to be married, and her wedding reception held on the lawn!

Larry gazed at the devastation, shaking his head, bewailing the required compromise of his newly acquired pacifism.

'Stupid little buggers,' he said. An affectionate lament, if ever there was one.

My expectation – based on my own conspicuous success in not catching moles – was, of course, that he would simply clear the displaced soil at a molehill, find the tunnel with his fingers and sink a trap into position.

'That's the last place!' Larry made no attempt to hide his amusement at my townee reasoning. 'The very last place.'

For a long time he looked at the evidence of this underground industry, the molehills zigzagging, as far as I could see, with neither rhyme nor reason.

'Females,' he said, 'bloody females; they never seem to be able to make up their minds, this way or that. Now males, they always tunnel in a straight line, shortest route from A to B. But females! Look at those.' He pointed at the heaps of soil. 'All over the bloody place.'

He continued to look, for perhaps a minute, then suddenly started to dig, finding the tunnel in no time, bang on target. How did he do it? He said he couldn't explain; just knew, adding it was a matter of experience, nothing else. His work was unhurried, methodical, and completed, I must say, with the pride of a professional killer who nevertheless hated his work.

Need I mention, the lawn was its customary snooker-table self by the time of the wedding. And what a wedding!

In the village every bride has the option of being taken to and from the church in our community coach, driven by a bushy beard wearing a Victorian-style uniform which he paid for himself, a magnificent outfit competing with the gowns of the bridal party for admiration. And if we have a community coach driven by the most lovable eccentric in the entire village and district, we also have a community spirit, never better expressed or felt than at a wedding. Virtually everybody turns out, particularly if the bride is widely known through growing up among us.

The coach arrives at the house with an immaculate lawn. The horse prances, impatient to be off. The church bells go crazy in celebration. Villagers cluster at the gate, others line the road. The bride, solemnly radiant, her father proud as a peacock, climbs aboard. The bushy beard clicks his tongue, gently pulls on the reins, and the triumphant drive begins.

Knowing most of the onlookers by name, the bride shyly smiles, and waves her hand like royalty – all the way to the village green half a mile away, and beyond to the gate of the church. A child, beside herself with excitement, finds it impossible not to throw her handful of confetti, precipitating similar showers from other well-wishers, showers of what the archdeacon calls his 'pet hate', a lost cause if ever there was one.

The bride makes her way to the porch; her veil is finally adjusted by the maid of honour; and the entire village rises as the organ thunders out its welcome.

Community – community *spirit* – that's what it's all about, as genuine as its roots go deep. But I wonder for how much longer? People born and bred here are of necessity moving out, looking for work and somewhere to live. Commuters are moving in, inflating the price of every house and cottage available. And – to quote the reluctant mole-killer – 'the new 'uns don't mix with the old 'uns'; they keep themselves to themselves, treating the village as a sort of retreat or dormitory, content to take but give little in return, as little as makes no difference. The old spirit, he says, is on the way out.

I was inclined to agree, or at least understand the grouse in his voice – until the wedding. *That* hardly suggested the old spirit was even dying, let alone dead. But there again, maybe – a relative newcomer myself – I wanted to believe things weren't changing, not fundamentally, despite Larry's grumbling about townee sentimentalists spoiling

141

everything. Spoiling? Perhaps that's too hard. He just thinks too many of the newcomers deserve nothing better than strangling by their own romanticism about country living.

13

Catching moles and dipping sheep

What doesn't change is Larry's attitude to moles, the reluctance with which he responds to every request to clear them. The latest was from a farmer concerned about the tender roots of new-sown grass. Larry set his traps, nine in all, and asked if I'd like to go with him to check the catch.

We drove a mile or so out of the village, and tramped to the first of two distinct clusters of molehills either end of the field. I carried a spade, Larry his gun. As we neared the first pile of soil, he signalled to tread warily *behind* him. Ten strides or so away he stopped, his eyes darting from one molehill to another. Walking as though on eggs, he positioned himself at one, watching, he'd previously explained, for the slightest movement of the soil, evidence of a mole still digging. I saw nothing. He raised his gun to his shoulder, waited . . . waited; and fired. From the molehill he picked up his first victim.

I was amazed. Consider for a moment. The molehill was as big as a large dinner plate. How come he never missed his tiny target? It was simply a matter, he said, of watching for movement in the soil, and working out the relative position of the mole.

'I only fire when I'm sure,' he said.

He handed me the mole, inviting me to feel how it wasn't possible to rub against the grain of the fur either way – the main reason, he explained, why the little creature could move backwards as fast as forwards.

'Speedy little bugger.' His voice was full of affection. 'In water too! Some day I'll catch one alive – it's not difficult! – and let you see how fast it can swim.'

The corpse was still warm. I felt its claws – 'pneumatic drills', as Larry described them – capable of digging beyond sight of a predator in no time; and I lingered over my examination of its minute eyes almost totally hidden beneath the fur, and not, according to Larry, very efficient. As a sort of compensation, he said, its senses of smell and hearing were particularly sensitive, the snout incredibly so. When it was investigating, or on the alert, either hunting or being hunted, extra blood was pumped into its snout, causing that area to swell and bringing into operation a network of nerves to the brain, enabling it to pick up the slightest movement, even air moving along the tunnel through being disturbed by the tiniest of creatures.

'With a nose like that,' Larry laughed, 'who needs eyes?'

He set more traps, and we moved to the other end of the field to check the ones put down the day before. Each of the first six contained a corpse. The seventh was not triggered, causing Larry to wonder whether he'd chosen the right place. The eighth contained a corpse. The ninth was missing altogether.

'The work of a badger!' the mole-catcher said; and started to poke around. 'It won't be far away, trap and mole, I shouldn't wonder.' He sounded light-hearted.

And so it proved. The bulging trap was lying by a gate.

'The mole gets caught,' Larry explained, 'the badger smells the mole, digs it out, trap and all; and usually decides it's too sour to eat, too bitter. Even foxes don't eat moles,' he went on. 'Proof enough of the terrible taste.'

Now I *was* in a quandary! To contradict such a knowledgeable countryman was out of the question. Yet nagging at the back of my mind was something I'd read in my BB (badger bible), an unequivocal statement that badgers ate moles. No question! Could Larry be mistaken? He was emphatic on the subject.

'Never mind badgers and foxes,' he said. 'Even crows and bloody magpies won't touch 'em; eat any carrion normally, but not moles!'

And then I remembered. He was absolutely right about foxes; at least foxes. For though I couldn't speak from first-hand experience, I knew that an acknowledged expert had made the same point: moles were not commonly eaten by foxes; a researcher had found only two examples in more than five hundred stomachs; and when four captive fox cubs were each presented with a mole, three promptly buried theirs, while the fourth ate one foreleg and shoulder, which it vomited a few minutes later.*

Could Larry be right about badgers too, despite the accredited experts?

Meanwhile, this irrepressible countryman continued his running commentary on the mole, more a panegyric in the circumstances. Moles were loners, fearsomely independent. Even in the breeding season there could be no guarantee that a fortuitous meeting of two moles of the opposite sex wouldn't result in a fight to the death! Most of the time, the males and females lived apart, but if their ways crossed, the fur, grain or no grain, began to fly in no uncertain terms.

'Vicious little buggers,' Larry characteristically summed up, affection still uppermost.

As for his claim about badgers not eating moles, about moles being ignored as carrion by wildlife generally, he told me a week or so later that the eight corpses we'd left in a pile on the edge of the field were still there, positive proof

* *The Red Fox*, by H. G. Lloyd (Batsford, 1981, p.72)

they were obnoxious to badger, fox, crow, magpie and everything else!

Could this be the case?

There wasn't, however, the slightest doubt about this deep-dyed countryman's respect – that's the essential word – *respect* for not only the mole but wild animals generally, even those categorized as pests. He couldn't, though, abide sentimentalists who tended to treat animals including farm stock as two- or four-legged humans. At least, this was my impression, until he introduced me to another undoubted countryman, a close friend of his, whose attitude was somewhat different. Or was it? Judge for yourself.

I first met him through Larry's invitation to watch sheep being dipped at the farm of the old man who, you remember, finally confessed about the public right of way and the gate on his land into the woods. It turned out to be quite a day, for other than the dipping! Misunderstanding the time, I arrived much too early, to find the old farmer waiting in the farmyard for an ambulance. There'd been an accident, blood everywhere.

We watched the ambulance speed past the turn-off to the farmyard, and I was dispatched to locate it and act as guide.

This little drama resolved, I went in search of Larry, who was pruning trees on the other side of the village. And there he was, halfway up an ash, manipulating his saw with the same expertise he brought to any one of his dozen crafts.

His employer for the day, owner of the sheep to be dipped, was kneading the ears of four or five bullocks as though each animal was a favourite pet, and whispering endearments as all of them jostled for prior consideration. Larry's face was a study, a picture of mischievous tolerance.

'He has a name for each of them,' he called across. 'Treats 'em like members of the family.'

The man doing the kneading laughed his agreement, not in the least embarrassed, on the contrary happy to concede that this was how he felt.

'I buy 'em as calves,' he said, 'and keep 'em till they're ready for market.'

'Don't they look good!' shouted Larry.

They did; very good. But my ex-townee mind was already trying to reconcile the depth of the kneader's affection with that ominous word *market*. I had every reason to appreciate that countrymen weren't sentimental about selling their stock for the best possible price; but surely in this particular case, bearing in mind the degree of attachment and personal involvement, *market* must mean a hell of a parting?

Only recently Larry had told me about a thirteen-year-old ewe, savaged as a lamb by a rogue dog, its teats torn off, its life saved by nursing from the farmer's wife, still living on the farm from which, she insisted, it would go only over her dead body! And *she* was a farmer's daughter as well as a farmer's wife, imbibing country unsentimentality with her mother's milk!

So how come this lover of his bullocks was so matter-of-fact about their sale for slaughter, as matter-of-fact as another farmer I knew who spoke of *getting rid* of an infertile bull? I would have asked him there and then, but he was already walking away to check his sheep for dipping.

At the dip I tied up my dog out of sight at an appropriate distance, and waited for the sheep, arriving in dribs and drabs, driven on by the bullock-lover, Larry and a retired shepherd happy to lend a hand for the morning. No sheepdog? And one was clearly needed, that much was

147

increasingly evident. Take it from me, sheep can be awfully independent without a sheepdog to keep order.

Eventually this lot entered the fenced area adjacent to the dip, meaning it was now necessary for them to enter one door of an outbuilding to emerge from another in a single-file approach to the dip itself. At the first door the leading two or three stopped as though its wide-open welcome was impassably barred, and wouldn't budge, like sentinels keeping the others out.

The bullock-lover told them not to be silly buggers.

The retired shepherd waved his armed and shooed.

Larry threaded his way through the now congested flock, grabbed the one nearest the door and heaved it through, a kick up its backside to help it on its way. The rest, as is the manner of sheep, immediately followed, fighting to be first!

Theoretically all we needed to do now was watch the sheep plunge in at one end of the dip and scamper out at the other! But, as I say, they can be awfully bloody-minded. To get them to the brink was relatively easy, with Larry providing the required propulsion, but the actual plunge, never mind their frantic efforts once in to get out, was something else. Again the theory was to keep them in and push them under – a thorough soaking – with the aid of a ducking crook, nothing to it, nothing at all; but after the first two or three had indulged their triumphant non-cooperation, it was decided that Larry and the ducking-crook operator should change places.

My job was to restrict the dripping sheep to a concrete area from where the pungent formalin could run back into the dip, releasing them in ones and twos as crowding from the other end demanded. Give 'em plenty of time to dry off, I was told, otherwise the cost of dipping was likely to be even more than an average sixty pence a sheep!

'Nothing's cheap these days,' the farmer who owned the

dip groaned. Fortunately, this didn't apply to his whispered running commentary as he stood by me, out of earshot of the others. Wonderful village gossip. Nothing vicious or scandalous, you understand. Just the inside knowledge of a villager who'd lived hereabouts for eighty years, and knew more than enough about everybody within miles.

All too soon, as far as I was concerned, the last sheep were through, and I found myself invited to join the others at the bullock-lover's place for a sandwich lunch prepared by his wife. The prospect was doubly appealing because it offered me the opportunity to ask her about the proposed removal of headstones from the chapel graveyard. She, I didn't doubt, would have details at her finger tips, for her practical devoutness was one of the main reasons the village chapel remained a centre of activity.

But first we had to get the sheep back to pasture, still without a dog. I collected mine, and fell in with Larry as the retired shepherd was doing his best to hasten our luncheon appointment. At this rate we'd starve to death!

Even so, when I told or rather reminded Larry that my dog was a trained sheepdog, it never crossed my mind he'd put two and two together with his customary alacrity. The sheep were all over the place. My dog was walking to heel. Ears pricked. Tail low. Eyes riveted on the sheep.

'What are you waiting for?' he said.

Hurriedly I explained I'd never worked her. She'd lived on a sheep farm until her retirement, and come to me only recently. Admittedly I'd often seen her work, and knew the commands, but obviously this didn't come within miles of actually working her myself.

The sheep were still pleasing themselves. Lunch beckoned. My dog looked from me to the sheep, from the sheep to me, clearly keen to work, baffled why I was taking so long to give the first command.

149

'Go on,' said Larry.

In a voice strangely unlike my own I whispered, 'Come bye.' The dog was off to my left like a rocket, nice and wide, round the back of the sheep, which immediately panicked at her enthusiastic approach. 'Lie down,' I shouted. The sheep steadied, then began to move in the right direction. The dog came on, again keen, too anxious to get back into harness, too rusty to function with her erstwhile independence; looking to me for command. The sheep again scattered.

'Lie down,' I repeated.

The old shepherd was incredulous, and remarkably tolerant. 'A trained sheepdog!' he called, apparently impressed by a dog whose only need was for a competent handler.

'Away to me,' I shouted. And her response was immediate, too quick for the sheep. Steady. STEADY. She crouched, her nose on her front legs, her eyes, strong as steel, on the sheep. Suddenly she sprang forward and nipped the nearest backside, setting the flock charging again.

'Lie down,' I screamed; grateful the leading bunch was moving in the desired direction. Within a minute or so they were back to pasture.

I knew I'd let the dog down, been unworthy of her skills and long working experience, but my embarrassment tinged with shame was jubilant, the very opposite of wretchedness. Retired she might be, away from sheep for some four years, accustomed to leisurely walking rather than speedy outbursts in response to her old shepherd's commands; but her class was self-evident, an eager talking-point as we made our way to the bullock-lover's cottage.

Headstones removed from the chapel graveyard?

repeated the devout one among us. Only the really old ones reaching back beyond anybody's concern, she explained. The problem was, they were littered all over the place, making it almost impossible to keep the surrounds neat and tidy, never mind the difficulties of cutting the grass.

Immediately there flashed to memory the solitary sheep and her lamp cropping the church graveyard, admittedly without ecclesiastical permission, having broken from their pasture next door, but most effective none the less. I never could understand why this was frowned upon, and the fence speedily reinforced. Surely a four-legged lawn mower was the answer?

Undeterred by the apparent incompatibility of such an idea and a sense of reverence, I gratefully changed the subject by asking about the bullocks going to market.

'No problem at all,' their owner laughed. 'While they're with me, I give 'em a good life, the best of everything. I reckon they owe *me* something.'

Larry's face was a study.

'That's as may be.' His eyes twinkled mischievously. 'But when the transporter arrives I've noticed you never seem to be around!'

'Sentiment ain't sentimentality,' protested the gentle bullock-lover. His wife nodded.

And recalling the endless ear-kneading and the way each bullock was addressed by name, I too could only nod.

14

Rook pie and the extraordinary cat-lover

I'm not so sure, though, about the taste – literally the taste! – of the retired major who lives in the big house beyond the nobs' end of the village. He's part of a syndicate for rearing and shooting pheasants, a group of mainly city-based men who come and go by stealth, judging by how little we see – as distinct from hear – of them.

Actually, this syndicate was recently disbanded for financial reasons, paradoxically the explanation we're now given for the sudden sparsity of game birds in and around the woodland. But none of this had anything to do with my doubts centred upon the major's taste.

The story was told to me by an Irishman whose job it was to 'lay down' the pheasant chicks in anticipation of the annual shoot. Job satisfactorily completed, he was invited to the big house, where the major, a generous host, was waiting. Inevitably the conversation was of game birds, of celebratory dinners they provided for gunmen and beaters alike; and this led the major to confess what the Irishman found barely credible. His first preference was not pheasant. Or grouse. Or partridge. Neither turkey nor chicken. All very pleasant, but lacking the essential flavour of his favourite.

He led his guest to the deep freeze, and pulled out a couple of rooks. *Rooks*.

'These,' he said. 'Simply beautiful.'

The Irishman wasn't sure how to react. Was this a come-on for his special benefit? Or could it be that the major, usually conscious of his dignity, was speaking nothing more (or less) than the simple truth? The Irishman stifled a belly laugh, still not convinced his leg wasn't being pulled. And murmured the mildest scepticism. Rook before pheasant?

'A most pleasing flavour,' reiterated the major. 'You really should try it!'

'And did you?' I asked.

'Not bloody likely,' he said.

I told the story next time I dropped into the village pub for a ploughman's, wondering whether rooks for dinner pointed to the origin of the old nursery rhyme '. . . four-and-twenty blackbirds baked in a pie'. The theme of edible meat guaranteed a lively session, aided by an old wag who claimed he'd heard on the radio that the latest craze in London was crocodile steaks, five quid a pound at posh shops. What really brought the discussion alive, however, was horse meat!

You might have guessed, we don't have too many horses in our neck of the woods; a few for riding, none for working. At one time the neighbourhood was reputedly full of them, pulling waggons, ploughs, a few carriages; but this was before the wholesale mechanization of agriculture. These days the only shire and heavy horses we see are showpieces!

Insisting he was being strictly logical, the old wag said the only way to stop the disappearance of the horse was to eat 'em! The French ate horseflesh like we ate beef and mutton. The only difference was our bloody stupidity; and he went on to claim that during the war, and probably now, we ate it unknowingly.

'With all the rationing,' he said, 'don't tell me we didn't sometimes get horse meat! Like in some restaurants now,' he added.

The barman contributed his considerable authority to the discussion.

'When the missus and me were in France on holiday, we tried it. Tasty. Snails, too.' His wife's face registered disagreement. 'It's all in the mind,' he told her. 'You eat pork. Don't tell me a pig's cleaner than a horse! And what about a cow wallowing in all that shit? A horse is hygienic by comparison.'

Maybe. But I couldn't let him get away with indicting the pig. Dirty animal? I knew otherwise. Given the chance, it kept its bedding area scrupulously clean, dry and sweet-smelling. Pigs were only dirty, I said, when they weren't looked after properly.

A pigman at the bar laughed out loud. 'You wouldn't think so if you saw the swill they eat on a smallholding too near my back door. Pigs! They'll eat any bloody thing, turn it into the finest pork in no time. It don't matter what they eat,' he summed up, 'it's what they turn it into that matters!'

Inevitably, living where we do, the conversation switched to a pig farm some six miles and three villages away. Even to drive past it was, I conceded, a question of holding your breath through a near permanent corridor of stench.

'Lovely,' said the pigman. 'Keeps me young and healthy. Puts hairs on your chest!'

And chuckling at his own earthy humour, he made off for a game of darts.

I, too, made off, towards another badger sett I thought of as peculiarly my very own. True, a handful of trusted enthusiasts now knew about it and took every opportunity to share my watching, but this did nothing to diminish my sense of personal possessiveness following its discovery after a long search.

I never arrived, not that day. No more than half a mile from the pub, a car drew alongside, and the village policeman wondered whether I'd heard about the trouble a farmer in the next village was having with badgers. They were taking lambs! He sounded more than merely suspicious.

Now I'd heard that rogue badgers – injured or too infirm for normal feeding – were sometimes guilty, but the number of confirmed *killings* as distinct from carrion findings was minuscule, sufficiently inconsequential to make me sceptical. I decided to approach, as it were, the horse's mouth.

My knock was answered by the farmer's wife. 'Badgers!' she said. 'No, not badgers. Mink!'

Once before, I'd heard such a claim, again from a sheep farmer's wife who insisted that mink were definitely the culprits, proved by the carnage. 'Have you,' she had asked, 'ever seen the work of a mink?' I'd admitted my ignorance. 'Our dog' – her eyes had blazed – 'cornered one in the coal house a few days ago. When I went out to investigate the commotion, I could barely believe it. Terrifying. The mink was spitting at the dog like an infuriated cobra, spitting and snarling.

'Wisely the dog kept her distance; just stayed at the door preventing escape. I ran for help. And even one of our men didn't find it easy!'

'But mink killing lambs?' I'd gently persisted.

She'd been emphatic. 'They bite the neck, bloat themselves on the lamb's blood. Horrible things! You should see the *carnage*.'

Now here was a second independent source, also an eyewitness, confirming how the killing was done.

'Any trouble from badgers?' I enquired.

'Never,' she said, 'not to my knowledge; only mink and, of course, foxes. My husband dug out a vixen not long ago, before she whelped; he knew she'd be a menace if she was feeding cubs. But he doesn't like to interfere, even with foxes. Now mink . . .'

It puzzles me why some people appear anxious to give the badger a bad name. An old countryman, for instance, reminiscing about the village forty-odd years ago, told me he'd found a badger in his henhouse, corpses all over the place; and killed it with one mighty blow on the head.

Ever since, nothing has touched his certainty that *all* badgers kill chickens!

He also told me of discovering the work of a fox in the same henhouse, every bird dead, only one missing. Beside himself with anger and hatred, he laced two corpses with strychnine, for the first time in his life not begrudging a fox a banquet on his chickens. Within the hour his own dog was dead.

Why, nevertheless, should he incorporate the badger in his understandable detestation of the fox? Understandable, that is, in the circumstances. My own affection and respect for Reynard remain undimmed.

Poison, I don't doubt, must often kill other than the intended victim. Or if not kill, make desperately ill. I came across the latest case in the village through making enquiries about a kitten, though the inadvertent poisoning involved a dog, and led me to the discovery of an unsuspected badger sett!

It all started when our eldest granddaughter arrived for the weekend. Could I, she wanted to know, find her a ginger kitten; it had to be ginger. Her boss was frantic for one, a replacement for the beloved that had dominated her life. Given longer notice, I could have asked around, but

156

the request seemed a bit unrealistic, until I remembered a postcard in the village shop offering four kittens to good homes. Even so, a ginger?

With granddaughter as escort, I knocked on the old lady's door, a cottage on the boundary of the next village. A massive ginger cat flashed past.

'No, not a ginger *kitten*,' the old lady lamented. 'But the lady next door, she might have one; has lots of cats, all colours.'

I knocked. The door was opened, and immediately I was swamped by cats, legions of all sizes, shades, even shapes. The lady's eyes began to water; she fought back the tears. Yes, she had a ginger kitten. But the thought of parting . . .

Somewhat surprised, I tenderly wondered whether the other twenty-five felines might be enough. What was one among so many? Such was my insensitivity to the essential nature of the true cat fanatic!

After many assurances, and promises of regular reports, we eventually came away carrying a sort of mobile luxury home, the lady's cat cage for journeys to the vet. When I returned it the next day, she was clearly distressed; she'd been awake all night worrying that the kitten might get lost in the busy streets of London. The thought of what might happen *then* she found unbearable.

I could only reassure her.

I gather she spends about £20 a week on cat food, and a small fortune at the vet's, no expense spared. Need I mention, her gentle husband is most tolerant; every time he sinks into his favourite chair he finds himself inundated with cats.

As though to confirm I wasn't yielding to fantasy, I shortly afterwards noticed a *situations wanted* advertisement in a national weekly:

SINGLE LADY, 43 (ex-librarian, French graduate) with thirty-six delightful pet cats, seeks permanent position (librarian? maid?). Suggestions welcome. Two secure catproof rooms, plus cooking facilities, sought. Details of (gross) wages and accommodation appreciated.

The cat-lover, calling at our cottage a few days later to enquire about Ginger – calling, by the way, with a massive bunch of chrysanthemums grown in her own garden – told me of another love in her life. A stray dog. It turned up on her doorstep, and, with the wisdom of its breed (collie), refused to go away. The resident dog, normally aggressive to other canines, wagged a greeting, then an enthusiastic welcome, and in no time the pair of them were installed at the hearth – needless to say, with the collusion of the lady of the house.

Naturally she went to the police, phoned the RSPCA, asked around, left no stone unturned. But – oh! – the relief when the newcomer wasn't claimed. So the two dogs and legions of cats settled down to their domestic bliss.

Then came that unforgettable afternoon.

The ex-stray was found in a state of collapse, clearly more dead than alive.

The gentle vet diagnosed a heart attack; prescribed tablets; intimated the wisdom of preparing for the terminal. A second visit the next day confirmed the prognosis.

What was she to do? Simply wait for the end? Was it conceivable the vet was right? He was, she conceded, a pleasant enough man, very thorough, well-meaning; but not a patch on his counterpart some ninety miles away where she used to live. If only . . .

Her husband backed their car out of the garage; she settled with the ex-stray cradled in her arms, and willed the miles behind her.

The vet took one look at the dog. Poisoning, he said, no

158

doubt about it; probably contaminated bait of some sort. The only hope, he explained, was an immediate blood transfusion. He continued to examine the dog, all the time thinking aloud, trying to reassure the agitated woman without raising false hopes. The problem was, he whispered, he had no blood in stock!

She didn't hesitate. No, not to give her *own* blood, as though you could share my stupidity!

Back to the car, a round trip of 180 miles to collect and deliver the other dog; and within days the two of them were once more snuggling by the hearth, their twenty-odd feline companions doubtless grateful to get back to normal.

As I listened to the story, I could hardly fail to notice that the whole episode was being relived; tears misted the teller's eyes, and finally rolled down her cheeks; only her radiant smile throughout leaving me in no doubt about the happy ending.

Just in case you're wondering, I should mention that this villager is the opposite of neurotic. Or let me put it this way. If *she* is neurotic, the sooner we all share her maladjustment the better.

Which brings me to the unsuspected badger sett!

I asked her if she ever saw badgers near her cottage. Not for a long time, she said. In fact, she'd never seen them, only heard there might be a sett; and she pointed to the woods far beyond her neighbour's cottage – up an incline, through a field with a public right of way, into a strip of woodland that snaked back on itself.

'You can't miss the woods,' she said, underestimating my ineptitude in such matters; but as for the sett itself, she couldn't, she underlined, be sure it was there at all.

Badger enthusiasts will confirm that searching for a sett is exciting and almost as satisfying as finding one. Looking for clues – runs often clearly defined by constant use, pieces of hair caught in a fence, dung pits, trees marked by badger claws, play areas of flattened bracken or grassland, upturned cowpats (beetles are the attraction), signs of nosing for worms, and of course the entrance or entrances themselves, frequently with evidence of recent digging (by badgers!) and bedding, either the old brought above ground to air or the new waiting to be taken below. There are farmers who might also point to flattened oats and barley or a diminished maize yield!

On this occasion, however, the woods were adjacent to pasture, not a sign of a plough anywhere. My dog and I eventually scoured the area, though at times she was wise enough to leave me to tread my way through the heavy undergrowth, making detours via easier terrain and waiting impatiently at the other end. As for the badgers, not a single indicator.

All that remained was a strip of woodland that truly snaked back on itself. I wasn't optimistic. Trees were sparse, and part of it ran parallel to the public right of way, near enough to persuade any badger seeking peace and quiet to reside elsewhere. So the first possible entrance I stumbled across merely fuelled my scepticism. A fox's earth? Even a rabbit's warren? Though the hole maintained its diameter as deep as I could see inside. In any case, usual badger signs were conspicuous only by their absence. If badgers were hereabouts, why no runs or dung pits?

Two more similar holes a minute's walking distance away did nothing to erode my disbelief. I spotted what looked like a run, decided it led nowhere, and pretty well accepted my search was in vain. Either I had misunderstood the cat-lover's location of the sett, or the badgers had moved out long ago.

And that, I suppose, would have been that, apart from

the behaviour of my dog. I turned to see why she was lingering, and spotted her sniffing with relish. Strolling across, I hardly needed to ask why.

A dung pit. Recently used. What is it, I wonder, that gives animals such ecstasy on such occasions? My highly intelligent sheepdog, fastidiously clean, appeared to be engaged in deep-breathing exercises, each more satisfying than its predecessor. Intrigued by the scent? Working out the identity of the depositor? Or is it that what we find so objectionable is somehow transmuted by sensitivity of smell in the so-called lower animal kingdom?

All I can be sure about is that my dog's obvious pleasure alerted me to the presence of badger or badgers in the immediate vicinity; and a little more searching was all that was required to lead me to the sett – a solitary entrance; at least, I couldn't find any more nearby. But I didn't doubt that this was the home of a badger or badgers, for – apart from confirmatory signs – I now knew that single-entrance setts weren't all that unusual. True, I hadn't come across one before, though I suspect that in my very first searching days I'd turned away from single-entrance setts, supposing them to be earths or warrens. This one left me in no doubt at all after I'd found footprints in the mud:

Male   Female

Understandably in celebratory mood, I made my way home by the river, spotting a heron fishing – though it took off long before I could get close – any number of pied wagtails, sixteen swans, and a family of ducks which to my inexpert eyes looked like gadwalls.

At our cottage, barely inside the door, a knock indicated the unexpected arrival of Larry, dropping in for a coffee on his way to thinning a wood two villages away. But dropping in for a purpose!

In the woods yesterday, he said, early afternoon, he'd spotted a badger; surprising enough in itself in bright daylight, but this one was unique in Larry's experience for a reason he could neither initially understand nor finally quite believe. The badger was the wrong colour; unmistakably a badger, but no white stripes and altogether darker. Almost black.

As he watched this enigma trundling towards him along a firebreak, he realized that what he called 'the poor old badger' was absolutely covered with something it found obnoxious, a pitiable sight, like a skunk trying to escape its own stink. Larry poked around and made three discoveries. First, a farmer was spraying slurry – more simply understood as concentrated animal dung and urine – gallons and gallons of the stuff. Second, much of it was running into the river. Third, field and river bank saturated, the farmer was spraying the rest of his load straight into a hole adjacent to the woods, an entrance to an extensive sett deep into the woods themselves.

You can imagine!

Badgers hate anything that contaminates, hate it even more than they love food. I remember a man complaining to the badger group to which I belong that badgers were ruining his garden, eating the lot, never mind their nosing for worms and the like. Our chairman, unsung badger expert beyond our part of Kent, sympathetic to the frustrated gardener, protective of the badgers, simply soaked rags in dirty diesel oil, and placed them at the point of entry. The badgers cleared off. Not that this method is infallible; badgers can be mightily persistent if food is their reward. But it does illustrate that these fastidiously clean animals are deterred by nothing more than filth.

So a sett filled to overflowing with slurry was a permanent eviction order. The irony was, the farmer meant the badgers no harm! Any more than he intended to contaminate the river. And Larry wasn't the only one who was furious. The neighbouring farmer was beside himself, concerned not only about the badgers and the river, but the bad reputation such a man was giving to the whole of farming, providing ammunition for conservationists!

Larry couldn't decide whether the slurry dumper was stupid, thoughtless or a secret hater of badgers. Not that this made any practical difference. The contaminated badger, like any others that managed to escape, was homeless, evicted despite the law.

We're simply hoping that the earful the offender received on this occasion – not least from his farming neighbour – might prohibit such callous behaviour. But we're not too optimistic. Anybody who can deliberately fill a badger sett with slurry is, we suspect, capable of pretty well anything.

It was so nice the very next day to meet his total contrast, in the backyard of a house on the outskirts of our nearest town. Charlie – well into his seventies, straight as a beanpole – doesn't claim to be a countryman, not in more than spirit. He asked me, for instance, if I'd seen the previous night's wildlife programme on TV – a python climbing a tree towards a rat's nest; four baby rats, eyes not yet open, instinctively aware of danger, clinging to their mother's back as she climbed to safety?

'Imagine how many hours of discomfort,' he enthused,

'those cameramen must have suffered; and all we had to do was sit back in comfort – put our feet up and watch! Some people grumble' – he sounded incredulous – 'about the price of a TV licence. That one programme was worth every penny!' He chuckled. 'Why travel to the ends of the earth, when you can see everything at home from an easy chair?'

Nevertheless, if he isn't exactly an adventure-loving countryman, out and about to see for himself at first hand, content to watch the badgers captured on film by Stephen King for TV rather than share a vigil at a sett not all that far from his urban situation, he does keep chickens in the backyard. Special chickens, a breed by the name, I believe, of Plymouth Rock. He told me they lay well, but make – as he puts it – bloody awful mothers.

Perhaps he was being unfair. You see, he put nine *duck* eggs under one, and she proceeded, one by one at daily intervals, to eject them from the nest, all but the last. Her devotion to this loner was absolute, and in the fullness of time a duckling almost emerged. I say *almost* because the birth was somewhat delayed; Charlie could hear tapping inside the egg and eventually see a tiny crack in the shell, but after a further thirty-six hours he decided if he didn't help, the prisoner would never escape.

Ever so gently he prised open the shell. Out popped the duckling, looking more dead than alive, and Charlie found himself joyfully functioning as a sort of life-support machine – an excellent one, too, judging by the speed with which the duckling achieved independence. The trouble was, the duckling grew – out of all proportion to a townee's sentimental anticipations or wishes! Convinced Charlie was its mother, the duck insisted upon remaining inside the house where it had been reared.

Actually, Charlie didn't mind all that much at first. He

said the duck was as companionable as a dog, and sufficiently different to be interesting. But unfortunately it proved to be fiercely resistant to house-training.

He keenly felt the duck was his responsibility. To wring its neck was out of the question. To give it away almost as bad. To expose it to the rigors of being a duck, taking its chance out of doors, unfair, evidence of a heartlessness Charlie didn't feel. Yet to keep it . . .

Eventually, at the end of his tether, eager to confirm that parting is such sweet sorrow, he agreed that his daughter, who had recently moved with her husband to a smallholding, should introduce it to half a dozen of her thoroughly undomesticated ducks. Not that this helped overmuch. A duck habituated to human company takes a poor view of its own kind, most of all when its freedom to associate domestically is suddenly removed. All hell was let loose. The former joy of Charlie's life wouldn't stop quacking, protesting that to be merely a duck after living like a human was intolerable.

So – the last I heard – it was being transferred to a deaf friend who had ducks of his own, and lived sufficiently distant from his neighbours to maintain their goodwill.

15
Women – the countryman's view

I must be careful what I say about marital relationships in the country, and the way the countryman evaluates women generally. It would be so easy to give the right impression.

An eighty-year-old horse dealer, for example, newly married again, said of his youthful bride: 'She's a lovely filly, I think I'll breed from her.'

A village butcher, too, not remotely wishing to insult his wife, other half of a devoted partnership, greeted his only customer by late morning: 'The only things moving in my shop today are the flies and my wife's tongue.'

Separated from tone of voice, dancing eyes, jovial laughter, such remarks could so easily be thought disrespectful, confirmation of lingering male chauvinism. The truth is that countrymen take their wives for granted no more than the average male, and only then in the sense of expecting them to fulfil the traditional role of domestic skivvy; plus, of course, to toil unpaid on farm or smallholding.

You see the danger! The countryman himself works hard, and assumes the same affliction or addiction in his wife. The result is that the women tend to be profoundly valued and outrageously taken for granted. Loved? No question. Cherished? Undeniably. Treated as indispensable? Beyond doubt. But both husband and wife will tell you there's little room for romance in farming these days. The drudgery involved, apparently never-ending, is as much emotionally as physically draining.

Consequently, a visiting city-lover might well ask, don't countrywomen feel exploited, taken for granted, treated

166

like chattels? There are some and some, but the vast majority, as far as I can see, would laugh at the very idea. No romance! Well, not if you judge by the average countryman's suspicion of public emotions. In this area he is quickly embarrassed, almost perverse in his anxiety not to reveal himself. The bullock-lover, you remember, felt justified in making the distinction between sentiment and sentimentality, yet even he viewed people with more heart than head as afflicted by fatal weakness, particularly if they were farmers permanently on the verge of ruin! Far better always to give the impression of being hard-headed, showing not the slightest suggestion of suffering from more heart than business acumen.

The same sort of approach applied to the countryman's attitude to ex-townees like me, and the far greater number of village commuters to the city. And if the newcomers happen to be women, they reinforce his prejudice in the sometimes crude ways he evaluates the opposite sex as a whole. He sees them in two distinct categories, categories into which they place themselves by their naked reaction to animals – domestic, farm or wild.

To rats, for instance.

This was illustrated at a large house on the boundary of the next village. But let me, first of all, declare my own prejudice. I called there shortly after newcomers from the city had moved in, simply to ask permission to follow a tip from a woodman about a reputed badger sett. It had been active when he was a boy!

The man at the door, friendly enough, was shifty, on the defensive, damning the badger with faint praise. He said he liked the animal, would do nothing, you understand, to harm it. But he still wouldn't let me examine the damage in his woods for which he claimed the badger was responsible.

'I only want to look,' I repeated.

He was emphatic, jokingly adding that badgers could be a nuisance at times!

Anyhow, this gentleman and his beautiful wife, both impatient to taste the fruits of country living as a contrast to their workaday world, installed themselves in their converted barn, and understandably – the palace smelling of new paint, pine wood, and no expense spared – decided to show it off to their city associates at a house-warming party.

Judging by the merriment through open windows, the occasion was a swinging success, guaranteed to convince the most confirmed city-dweller that living in the country was nothing if not peaceful. Highlight of the night was a tour of the house – exposed beams, open fireplace, large windows displaying fields and woodland; and (in some ways, most impressive of all) the fitted kitchen. Simply magnificent.

Ubiquitous cupboards, miles of worktops, a table specially made to evoke farmhouse atmosphere, a giant Aga – and an ingenious swivel cupboard. The merest touch swung it through 180 degrees, each spacious shelf immediately accessible. The hostess demonstrated. Gentle push. Round came the shelves. And there for all to see were the rats.

Only two. Nothing excessive. The pair of them were too busy gorging themselves to do more than scarper straight through the crowded legs of the galvanized onlookers.

According to my informant, the female screams were not unlike a bulling cow or crows cawing or sheep newly separated from their lambs.

Bedlam.

Terror.

You do see, though, what the countryman means about

women placing themselves into one of two categories by their naked reaction to animals!

Not all members of even the favoured category, it must be said, meet with the countryman's unqualified approval. An old villager, plagued by rats, desperate to get rid of them, nevertheless worried herself sick after learning from the pest-control officer, formerly the rat-catcher, that he intended to poison them. Couldn't he, she asked, exterminate them without doing them any harm?

She was no more approved of than a relative newcomer whose reaction to the discovery of rats in her cottage prompted her immediate return to an urban setting, presumably unaware that rats were as likely there. On second thoughts, perhaps 'as likely' is an overstatement. At a farm not a thousand miles from hereabouts, rats by the lorryload had to be removed, upwards of ten thousand corpses in all. The pest-control officer himself, hand on his heart, told me the story. No tears about that!

Unhappily, lifelong country dwellers no less than recent escapees from city and town can't always tell the difference between water voles and rats. In fact, water voles stick to river banks or sometimes grassland and, unlike rats, are solitary or members of small groups. To associate them with the detested and understandably dreaded rat is an injustice.

Take it from me, rats are no respecters of the most idyllic human setting. Shortly after we'd installed our half-dozen hens, automatic feeder in the henhouse constantly replenished, I noticed a hole in the floor. Mystified why I hadn't noticed it before, such was my inexperience, not to say stupidity, it never crossed my mind to do other than repair the damage.

The hole returned.

Grew bigger.

Strange, I thought.

Only sighting a rat disappearing under the henhouse alerted me to the reason!

The pest-control officer laughed his head off. Then he enjoyed a second and third cup of tea, reminisced about his judging at poultry shows all over the country, enthused about his collection of ancient farm machinery, enough to start his own museum, before comprehensively demonstrating why the rats didn't stand a chance. A true expert on the warpath.

He reminded me again that countrymen are born not made. I thought I was on my way to joining their number indistinguishably, but was compelled to accept that no matter how long I live in the country I shall remain essentially a city man; content never to see the city again, grateful to explore my new environment and, most of all, get to know countrymen and women, many of them as colourful in character as skilful in dying country crafts. But none of this, I now appreciate, will ever make me a true countryman, not after the fashion of the rat-catcher or Larry, the pacifist killer of moles, or the cowman who cares as much about the badgers on his farm as about his herd of Friesians, or a farmer and his wife, both in their eighties, who, still battling with an outside loo twenty strides or so from their farmhouse back door, would never dream of leaving for urban mod cons. Don't ask me why, after all these years, they haven't applied for a grant to remedy the situation. Lack of money to make their contribution? I doubt it. But one thing's for sure. They won't leave their farmhouse until carried out feet first.

Whenever I'm tempted to think I'm becoming a true countryman myself, I fortuitously bump into such people, and recognize that fundamentally we're as different as chalk and cheese. This very week I stopped to examine and admire the evidence of a master hedge-builder's recent work. The way he'd repaired and reinforced it, interweaving sturdy offshoots by half cutting the base and easing into place, encouraging new growth, all with the finish of a neatly packed parcel, compelled respect for a skill in danger of disappearing with an ageing generation.

Further up the bank I found the man himself at work.

'Time for a chat,' he said. 'Always time for a chat. Them that rushes get to graveyard first.'

He was from another village, had lived there all his life, apart from during the war – but that, he laughed, didn't count – he and his wife, in the same house, never wanted to move, couldn't afford to, anyway.

'Hedge-building and the like don't pay much,' he said. 'What I lose in me pocket' – he eyed me quizzically – 'I gain in peace of mind!'

No, he didn't possess a car; never had.

No, he wasn't much given to holidays. Two or three days at a time were enough for him, walking the fields with his dog, the pair of them sniffing around. 'Ain't much we miss between us,' he said. His wife sometimes went up north to see her sister; otherwise they both stayed put.

No, he didn't watch telly much. Preferred whist in the village hall a couple of nights a week, sometimes at home with a few friends, all of them over eighty, older than himself, one deaf and dumb, charming woman. Good player too!

He picked up his billhook, turned as though to start work, changed his mind and led me about a dozen strides to a tree with a hole six feet or so up the bole.

'See there,' he whispered.

I saw nothing.

'Stand on tiptoe,' he said.

A mallard sitting, just the crown of her head visible.

'She don't seem to mind me working.' His eyes shone. 'Knows I mean her no harm.'

And he tiptoed away, this time to resume building the hedge. 'By the way,' he called over his shoulder, 'do you play whist?'

I admitted my ignorance.

'Don't know what you're missing!' He slashed another offshoot and began to manoeuvre it into position.

It was, I suppose, his tenderness towards the sitting mallard that prompted me again to wonder about what governs the average country- or city-dweller's attitude to wild animals. Never mind the contrast of badger-baiters and badger-protectors, the controversy surrounding blood sports, the bitterness between animal-lovers and animal-exploiters, what ultimately accounts for individual kindness or cruelty? Even in the country we love the bluetit but hate the crow; swoon over the robin but detest the magpie; exterminate the rat but welcome the flea-ridden hedgehog, whooping like children if it takes up residence in our garden, killing it with kindness in the form of bread and milk.

Ah, yes, but the crow and the magpie and the rat are vicious! Which just goes to show how little we know about the bluetit and the robin and the hedgehog on the warpath, no less vicious in their own way. Ask their prey.

Even badgers occasionally stick their noses in where they're not wanted!

A farmer phoned the chairman of our badger group, miles from here, to say he was worried the sett on his land was likely to be a casualty as the bulldozers moved in, part of his plan to bring a corner of tatty woodland under the plough. The chairman, a well-known badger authority, scoured the area, talked unhurriedly with the farmer and concluded that the situation was critical – for the badgers. The only solution was to persuade them to shift their centre of activity; in a word, to get the hell out of it before their world literally caved in.

The farmer expressed his willingness to co-operate by postponing the bulldozer for a few days – even two or three weeks – but this flexible limit must, he underlined, be reasonable. No good expecting him to wait forever.

Once more the badger-group chairman reconnoitred the whole area, and from the centre of the sett marked every single entrance in concentric circles. His aim was to stink out the badgers, first from the outlying entrances and tunnels until only the central entrance remained unpolluted, then to make this last refuge progressively intolerable; giving the badgers themselves both time and inclination to transfer elsewhere.

Having settled his strategy, he worked out all the practical implications, leaving nothing to chance, and – knowing and supporting the law – applied for a licence to start the operation on behalf of a protected species.

Many miles removed from the actual field situation, the bureaucrats turned him down. It was, they said, too near the time for cubbing – something the chairman, needless to say, had *not* overlooked. Meanwhile the farmer, apart from grinding his teeth, was threatening to call in the bulldozer anyway.

So what to do?

But you do see why conservationists, often with the best will in the world, rub farmers up the wrong way, even farmers whose only wish is to co-operate.

16

A visit from an expert

Shortly afterwards the chairman of the badger group spent a Saturday with me, confirming that my enthusiasm wasn't running away with me in claiming discovery of one sett after another in our badgerless village – seven in all within easy walking distance of our cottage. It took a bit of believing. For a decade we'd lived in the village without even suspecting a single badger anywhere near, let alone a sett. Then paradoxically the dead badger had alerted me to the possible presence of living ones, more and more of them over the weeks and months, in places I thought I knew better than the back of my hand, actually in woodland through which I'd tramped a thousand times, unseeing of badgers or their signs. In retrospect, my blindness seemed incredible.

From my standpoint, Martin's coming couldn't have happened at a better time. Only a few days before, I'd been following up clues of another possible sett, on the other side of the road from the private wood in which I now knew, despite never managing to catch the countryman who repaired the fence around it and generally kept it in order, that badgers were in residence. I'd watched there myself; best proof of all.

The possible sett had tantalized me for ages. I mentioned in *The Grass is Greener* that I had watched there, too, but seen only a couple of foxes. Only! At the time, as now, this was reward enough. But not alas in terms of settling whether badgers were also in the vicinity. What added to my uncertainty was the occasion I rounded a bend in a firebreak near a couple of suspect entrances, and saw a fox cub dive into one; proof, I concluded at the time, that foxes not badgers were in residence. I belabour the point to illustrate how easily novice badger enthusiasts can misread the signs, assuming an earth is a sett, and vice versa.

On another occasion – I'd returned times without number, and remained unsure – I spotted the owner of the private woodland, pottering in her garden, and naturally we talked about badgers. She mentioned her free-range cats, joy of her life, and wondered about the safety of the badgers now they were venturing nearer the house, not from *her* wood, she said, but the one on the other side of the road!

There must be another sett not far away, she smiled.

I kept searching. And searching. Finding more entrances. Or earths? I was never absolutely sure. A whole summer passed, and we were well into winter before I discovered what was almost under my nose! In extenuation, I was previously at the right place at the height of summer, when bracken and other undergrowth made it devilishly hard to see with certainty the usual telltale signs. But *now* it was the end of January; bracken and the rest had fallen back, exposing a number of entrances, three positively in use, and recent digging on the mounds.

And yet and yet. A main sett? An outlier? I honestly didn't know, couldn't make up my mind. How nice that a real expert was soon to bring his vast experience to bear.

Martin arrived in his Mini, almost; having cast his eye over the track leading to our front door, he decided to park on the road before sploshing the rest of the way, complete with binoculars, camera, maps, compass, notebook, badger-group records, anorak, wellingtons, a hat as battered as mine, and a walking stick cum staff, perfect support in the kind of terrain we faced for the day.

Not wasting a second more than it took to drink two cups of tea, we made for the first of my queries, a sett I thought of as an outlier, but with lingering doubts that it was a sett at all. It was no more than five minutes' walk from our cottage. Martin's running commentary made me realize how much I knew – and how very much I didn't know – about natural history, and badgers in particular.

We crossed a field, and I pointed to a bank. Never mind the mud, the result of incessant rain for weeks, he was quickly on all fours, sniffing down a hole.

'Fox,' he said. 'But hang on . . .'

Still on his knees at another hole, he gently poked over the loosened earth, turning it over with the circumspection of a man searching for gold. And unwinding himself, all six foot three, his face a study of triumph, he held up to the light a single black and white hair. Then another. And a third. Proof positive of badgers, he declared. Often I myself had searched for such evidence, but always at nearby hedges and the bottom of fences. His search was concentrated at the entrances themselves, immediately inside and outside.

'Badgers,' he repeated.

But no sign of a dung pit, not beyond the one I'd found months before, which even then had little to suggest recent patronage.

'Perhaps the dung pits are underground,' he said.

I couldn't believe it! Dung pits underground? I thought badgers were fastidious in such matters, not a chance of them fouling their own living quarters.

'So they are,' he said. 'But this doesn't mean they invariably come above ground to crap. More often than not they do, no doubt about that, but sometimes presumably they find it convenient to stay below; the dung pits are well away from the main living area.'

I shouldn't have been so surprised, for Ernest Neal had made the same point in his seminal book on badgers, but I'd taken for granted he'd been referring to behaviour so atypical as to be virtually discounted.

'Not so,' said Martin. 'Evidence of dung pits underground is conclusive. You can be quite sure,' he added, 'that such pits neither inconvenience nor contaminate the badgers.'

He returned to the hole where he'd sniffed fox. Again he picked over the soil, and held up to the light first one hair then another. Both red.

'At least one fox in residence,' he declared. 'Perhaps a pair.'

So here at the very start of our day was confirmation – in our own backyard, as it were – that foxes and badgers tolerated each other in close proximity of earth and sett. Yes, but was this particular sett, I wanted to know, only an outlier, and if so how often was it used. When? Why?

Martin looked quizzical, smiled and admitted he didn't know, not for sure. A number of reasons were open to conjecture – transit sett, privacy for cubbing, standby sett for emergencies at the main sett, funk hole for victim of a dominant boar's displeasure (they fight among themselves, occasionally to the death), perhaps a varied combination of the lot. We could rarely be certain. No doubt, though, that this sett was occupied at the moment, for how long and precisely why was anybody's guess. By the look of things, it was used infrequently for limited periods. The only way to be sure was sustained observation for years rather than months!

We returned to the road. Not far along it I was able to point to the spot where I'd found my first badger, clearly killed by a passing vehicle. And I filled in the details, the haunting details, of how days later the badger appeared to be coming back to life – raised from the dead by a mass of maggots, the result of the greenfly thrusting her oviduct (egg-conducting tube) into an orifice (nose, eyes, mouth, wound) and packing it tight for two to three hours; then, her essential life's work completed, flying off to die. In next to no time, I told Martin, the badger was almost walking, animated by this squirming mass in Nature's great recycling process.

This brought to mind a similar story of his own, with a somewhat bizarre ending. He received an urgent phone call about a badger involved in a road accident, though the caller wasn't sure whether the animal was dead or alive. Martin approached it with due circumspection, aware from painful experience that the jaws and claws of even a stunned badger were capable of fearsome damage.

The pathetic creature moved, turning its head enough to reinforce caution. Martin crept nearer still, and saw the head again slightly move. He stood watching further minute tremors, all the time working out how best to safeguard himself from injury as he transported the badger to a vet. He knew the importance of grabbing the terrified animal so as to render it helpless and incapable of lashing out.

His aim was to throw his coat over the front half of its body, and in one lightning movement grab the snout and jaws before heaving the struggling mass under his arm and holding it like a vice.

Right. He was now within reach. Again the head moved. He hesitated for a moment to let the poor creature settle, eased forward, slowly lowered himself, and *grabbed*.

The head came apart in his hand, severed by the bluebottle's bloated progeny. And the stench! That's what he remembered most, badger's head in his hand or not.

He also mentioned that in picking up a badger it can be

178

helpful to dangle a blanket, which, once grabbed, as it most certainly will be, should be wrapped round the jaws and fore claws!

Incidentally, research based upon a thousand badgers killed in road accidents in the Home Counties and the South-West suggest that most such deaths occur during two peak periods – one in March, the other in July and August. Furthermore, the researchers believe that these two peaks are related to mating behaviour, which for some badgers involves lengthy journeys into little-known or completely new territory.

In other words, the badgers' seasonal sex drive and our roads are incompatible, even our lazy country lanes. All I can say is that if such an unhappy price for sensuous wanderlust doesn't encourage you to drive with added caution, nothing will!

We next cut across three fields to the wood containing what I continued to think of as my very own sett, and almost immediately saw ample evidence that if dung pits were sometimes underground, these first-love badgers of mine were disposed to relieve themselves in God's fresh air. One pit after another was overflowing, the dung new enough to be last night's.

At the sett itself, deeper into the wood and not far from the ruins of a farm worker's cottage not used since the early 1940s, entrances most in use were clearly marked by recent digging. Proudly I showed Martin the tree in which I'd perched for my very first badger-watch there, a tree still indicated by the old plastic oil container I'd found in the wood and placed by the tree to assist my return to the right spot. Take it from me, it isn't always easy to pick out a particular tree, not at first.

At that time, merely a couple of years ago, not another

soul knew about this sett, I emphasized to Martin, and even now no more than a handful of trusted villagers and friends shared the secret.

I glowed with humble pride.

He smiled, fiddled about in his anorak, and eventually pulled out a dog-eared sheet, which he continued to examine with the leisurely aplomb of someone who knew he wasn't mistaken.

'According to my records,' he said, 'this sett was reported to the badger group some fourteen years ago. One of our founder members used to cycle all over the place, miles from home, always on the look-out for badger setts. *He* found this one. That's right,' he again glanced at the paper, 'in 1974.'

'Is nothing sacred?' I asked.

My ego deflating by the second, we moved off towards what I anticipated would be the mystery of the day. Was it or wasn't it a sett? Main? Outlier? Earth? For there still niggled at the back of my mind remembrance of the fox cub diving into one of the entrances, despite recent indicators I'd found of badgers!

As we walked, wind howling, rain in heavy showers, mud often above our ankles, I was entertained and enlightened by one badger story after another, each evoked by my ignorance, my never-ending questions.

Did he, I asked, know anything at first hand about badger funerals?

His answer was to invite my interpretation of the following. At a sett he frequently visited, a smell from one entrance stopped him in his tracks. Its pungency indicated a decomposing body. Then why hadn't the badgers entombed the corpse and abandoned that part of the sett – a practice I've already mentioned?

A few days later he returned not only to find the smell

gone, but a grave nearby showing the outline of a badger, and badger body markings pressed into the soil to complete the burial. Martin himself didn't and doesn't doubt this admittedly only circumstantial evidence. How else, he asked, was the dead badger brought above ground? And what about those press markings in the soil at the grave?

I listened.

It's so hard to be absolutely sure.

But the next story he told me was simply dripping with proof, an eyewitness account with no possibility of mistaken interpretation. The badgers at one of his favourite setts, accustomed to his presence, accepted him as virtually a member of their social group, allowing him free access and finally appearing to ignore his nearness altogether. What also added to the appeal of this sett was its layout, or more accurately terrain. It was down a small quarry, and at times he was able to watch from a level lower than the badgers, near enough almost to gaze into their eyes.

On one occasion, sitting on a ledge which sloped down like a funnel, he was approached by a remarkably friendly and inquisitive sow cub, which – encouraged by his whispered endearments – squatted, looked over its shoulder as though to check it was precisely positioned, and proceeded to empty its clearly bursting bladder. The urine flowed along the funnel, into Martin's wellington boot and down his sock!

My utilitarian mind wondered why he didn't get out of the way. Perhaps nothing more than surprise? After all, it isn't every day a badger grants such distinction. Or was he sufficiently charmed by *all* the badgers to be slow on the uptake at the antics of this playful youngster? Whatever the reason, he reckons his left foot was awash with about a quarter of a pint. And such reckoning wasn't unscientific, for this expert's wish for substantiated evidence leads him to conduct badger post mortems. Naturally, among other things, he extracts the urine and measures it, the average amount suggesting that a full bladder contains in the region of a third of a pint, in this case confirmed by his wellington boot. At the next sett he visited, still wearing the unwashed sock, the badgers were not impressed! Strange really, for Martin himself claimed that the smell was only diabolical until he got used to it.

Such devotion to research was underlined by his response to my next query. Do badgers eat moles? I told him about Larry's claim. He refused to dogmatize, apart from saying, would you believe, that of all the dung pits he'd analysed only one sample had indicated mole!

'You scoop up the contents of dung pits?' I tried to sound casual. And didn't doubt I was in the presence of a dedicated badger man.

By now we were approaching the environs of the mystery sett. His eyes darted, picking up one run after another, a couple leading as clear as day across the disused track away from the main entrances. We followed them until they petered out, then retraced our steps, while he stressed how important it was I should renew the search at the first opportunity.

I led him to the hole into which I'd seen the fox cub dive; and another hole no more than six strides away, both heavily marked by recent digging.

Badgers, he said, with barely a second glance.

And in a flash he was again on his knees picking over the soil, gently, methodically, once more directly at the entrances. There were black and white hairs aplenty, he held one after another up to the light for me to see.

We – he! – found the dung pits.

Then a scratch tree.

Then any number of bluebells uprooted by the badgers to eat.

Then more entrances.

Then – a cry of triumph from him – a gall!

You don't know what a gall is? That makes two of us. Which made his excitement, not to say ecstasy, all the more unnerving. He was beside himself. Like a man finding gold. Assuring me this was his lucky day, purring like a cat full of cream, he dived into his anorak, adjusted the focus of his camera and started the clicking. Endlessly. This had to be the find of the century.

'What *is* a gall?' I intruded.

His snapping kept me waiting. The one thing I couldn't doubt was my privilege in sharing his serendipity. With the care of a surgeon, he removed one of the galls, leaving half a dozen or so, and cut it down the middle.

'There!' he indicated.

And I gazed. Clueless. Feeling alienated. His incredulity made me desperate to share it.

'You see,' he explained, 'the gall results from a gall-midge or gall-wasp laying its eggs on, say, a bramble, as in this case. The eggs are cocooned in these galls, which develop on the host plant. In the fullness of time, the larvae eat their way out, nourished by the galls, and eventually start the whole operation again. Remarkable, isn't it! Very unusual to find a specimen at all.' He handed me the cut gall. 'Especially as fine as this.'

I nodded agreement, popped the gall into my pocket, and wished I were a real countryman.

Martin was enthusiastic about the whole setting. It reminded him, he said, of a badger monastery he used to visit regularly. Eleven boars without a single sow!

'Pardon?' I said.

'Eleven boars,' he reiterated. 'A strictly male community, unique in my experience. I've never fathomed,' he admitted, 'why so many single-sex badgers should live together, certainly from November to the end of March. By then they were fewer in number, presumably in response to their urge to mate, but this doesn't explain why eleven boars should form a celibate community, not a sow in sight. Does it?'

I was suitably silent.

No less surprising was his next story, one running counter to my previous understanding. He told me that he himself had seen a badger enter a fox's earth, the vixen watching apparently helpless with fear, and from the earth heard squeals and the sound of crunching bones before the badger popped out with a dead cub in its mouth.

But I thought badgers and foxes were generally tolerant of each other! And what about the vixen? Surely in such circumstances she would fight, no matter how overwhelming the odds? And was the badger a rogue or an old-timer looking for easy food knowing this vixen wouldn't resist? Was it displaced aggression against a stronger boar in the sett? Or simply – as Martin himself suggested – a boar seeing the fox as either a nuisance or a competitor, perhaps a bit of both?

Who can tell? Such questions, however, add zest to my own watching. They also reminded Martin of a lady who came upon a fox and badger face to face and clearly spoiling for a fight, neither prepared to give ground. Her approach broke their trance-like preoccupation with each other, whereupon the fox scarpered while the badger, hyped up and nonplussed, rushed towards *her*. She too scarpered, and managed to slam her garden gate in its face. Martin asked her why she didn't hang about to see what happened!

Her reply is better imagined.

* * *

There remained two more setts I was anxious for the expert to see, one for confirmation or otherwise about badgers being in occupation, the other simply because it was rather special, easily the biggest in our badgerless village. Also, let me be honest, because his records didn't contain a reference to either, not a mention. But, first, a break for lunch.

Not that *he* did much eating. He was too busy telling me one fascinating badger story after another from his vast experience.

Had I heard about the young couple who spotted a badger lying in the *middle* of the road? They pulled their car to the side, saw the animal was terribly injured and promptly decided she would go for help while he – traffic flashing past in both directions – stood guard over the badger. By the time Martin, called out by the police, arrived at the scene, the badger was barely alive. After a lot of care, including force-feeding, the sow was still unable to walk – a sign of possible brain damage; but eventually not only did she recover completely but she dug her teeth into Martin's hand with too much enthusiasm in the process! She was returned to the scene of the accident and released.

Badgers, it seems, evoke all manner of reactions in members of the public. Another car driver was flagged down by a teenage horse-rider frantic about an injured badger cub she'd just found. Having expressed his indignation at being stopped, he actually tossed the cub over a hedge, climbed back into his car muttering uncompliments about the girl's sentimentalism, and drove away grumbling in unconscious irony that she might have caused an accident.

The next driver flagged down was the extreme opposite, sharing the horse-rider's desperation about the terrible injuries, and immediately rushed off to find assistance. This time the cub was collected by a vet and nursed back to fitness before being released to the wild.

Other stories had similar happy endings: of road victims, some nursed for weeks at an animal sanctuary in co-operation with the badger group, likewise released at the point they were found; of a large sow cub removed from a grain pit into which it fell – not unlike the intrepid rescuer, who at one point was standing on his head, stuck, unable to get out unaided – at two-thirty in the morning; of an irate badger-lover seeking the practical knowhow to safe-guard his garden from dung pits! As I say, one story after another until I began to worry we wouldn't get to the remaining couple of setts before dark.

The first was no more than seven or eight minutes' walk from the cottage, barely off the main road to the next village and tucked away in a few trees. I'd first come across it through a woodman working miles away who'd told me of seeing a badger dashing across the road there, and there had been other sightings by a married couple in the nearest house. They themselves admitted they wouldn't know how to recognize a sett if they saw one.

The woodman, by the way, some thirty years ago, at the age of fourteen, looked destined to become a carpenter; a refinement of his natural talent. Wood was the love of his life, its smell, its grain, its adaptability, most of all for the making of beautiful objects, the more complex the challenge the better.

But an apprenticeship, as he soon learned, involved other things, less exciting, like repairing chairs and cupboards, fixing doors, replacing floorboards. He was dispatched to this end to a grand hotel, at Brighton, I think he said, but no matter. The place was intimidating in its poshness; carpets everywhere, waiters immaculately dressed, with professional polish to match, grandiose dining room, receptionists and other staff deferential to each and every guest, the guests themselves clearly able to afford and expect the best. And the banister, smooth, inviting, all the way from top fifth to ground floors, a veritable Grand National course without the jumps, twisting from flight to flight, guaranteeing a speedy descent.

The temptation haunted him. All he had to do was cock a leg, hold tight and go!

He did, one morning, when nobody was about. Like a jockey, he went arse first, gathering speed, finally going like the clappers, without a brake.

The terminal point, a solid post with a carved pineapple magnificently on top, awaited. He hit it, to quote his less than accurate delicacy, *head on*.

Wallop.

The post splintered.

The massive pineapple fell like a head rolling from the guillotine.

Good job, too, he said, otherwise he might have lost at least his manhood!

As it was, the incident marked him in more ways than one. He also lost his job, and any hope of continuing his apprenticeship; but not his love affair with wood of any sort in any form. So he became a hurdle-maker, not to mention the many other crafts associated with a coppiced wood. He loved the life, the loneliness, the changing seasons, the smell of smoke rising like incense as he fulfilled his legal obligation to keep his working area neat and tidy.

But all this, as I say, was by the way. He told me in some detail about seeing the badger tearing across the road, the only sighting of his life, and asked me to let him know if I discovered anything.

'Funny thing,' he said, 'I don't see much wildlife in the

wood. You'd think, wouldn't you . . .' and went on to state the obvious.

It proved fairly straightforward to locate the sett, if such it was. What made me hesitate at the time and subsequently was my inexperience demanding more than the single entrance I could find in the thick undergrowth. Despite now knowing better, I still wasn't absolutely sure, not least because this solitary entrance seemed permanently blocked with last autumn's leaves and the like. Two other entrances I eventually discovered showed little indication of badger activity.

Martin decided almost at a glance. For a start he spotted another entrance with fresh digging, clearly exposed by the undergrowth falling back in winter; but conclusive proof came from his now familiar picking over the soil immediately outside the entrance – black and white hairs aplenty. And as though this wasn't enough, a dung pit overflowing from recent patronage.

With four of my setts already confirmed as active, another, like the one containing my first-love badgers, also recorded years before and still undoubtedly active, and a sixth at which proof was again my own watching, all that remained was the most extensive sett of all, badgers galore in residence. I knew!

En route for it the badger stories continued. Was I aware of the extent of badger-digging, not only in the Garden of England but all over the place? There had been recent court cases in Northumberland, Cumbria, Humberside, Greater Manchester, West Yorkshire, Worcestershire, Nottinghamshire, Staffordshire, Clwyd, South Glamorgan, Buckinghamshire, Essex, Hertfordshire, Avon, Lancashire, Merseyside, South Yorkshire, Derbyshire and, apparently worst of all, Cheshire. His special lament was, of course, reserved for Kent, where the latest case involved three men caught in the act at a sett on the outskirts of Dover.

Half the trouble, said Martin, was that the culprits, found guilty with no mitigating circumstances, were fined an average of £200, derisory as a deterrent, apart from being an insult to the badgers.

We crossed a precarious plank over a brook into the woods, the only way in, and recrossed it lower down, scrambling over a fallen tree, and . . . there it was, a sett impressive enough to excite the most experienced of badger-watchers. He stood gazing. Mumbling his delight. Wondering why his records contained not a mention. Assuring me this one sett alone had made his day.

Lightfooted as cats, we moved from one cluster of entrances to another, examined dung pits, scrutinized trees for scratch marks, followed runs deeper into the wood, some continuing on the other side of the brook, and located – my enthusiasm reinforced and given direction by his expertise – even more entrances than I'd ever suspected.

I pointed out the tree from where I watched, told him of the vixen and her four cubs playing to their hearts' content (presumably unaware of some badgers' partiality for fox cub meat); and – viewing the devastation from the October hurricane – discussed whether this or that fallen giant might serve as some sort of perch. To get aloft otherwise wasn't going to be easy. The only feasible standing tree for patronage, a magnificent oak, looked unscalable.

Despite failing light and faster falling temperature, we lingered, charmed by the silence of the wood, excited by indicators all over the place of badger occupation, soaking up the magic. Martin identified different trees, and the pair of us became increasingly conscious of their sinister outlines as the gloom thickened, the brook's babbling somehow accentuating the eeriness.

A wood in winter. Beneath us lay a labyrinth of tunnels with snug chambers accommodating sleeping badgers, some of them nearing their fullness of time for cubbing. Indeed, perhaps already some cubs had arrived, eyes closed for five weeks or more, skin with greyish-white silky fur, kept warm and suckled by devoted mothers, guarded with their life.

Soon – late April, early May – they would emerge for a whole season of black and white ballets, the best seats absolutely free.

'Have you,' Martin enquired, 'ever watched at this time of the year?'

I admitted I'd rarely seen a badger from late October to early spring; last time, exceedingly cold, I'd barely caught a glimpse of *one*. Almost a waste of time!

'*Now* can be a good time to watch,' he said. 'Cubbing below means that soon afterwards mating sometimes begins. You know the sow comes into season within days or a week or so of giving birth! Hectic time.' He laughed. 'Plenty of activity. Well worth the cold penetrating your bones. Mind you,' he added, 'you might see nothing. Nothing at all. But it's worth trying.'

We sauntered back to the cottage, too busy swapping experiences to notice puddles and mud in the darkness. Then, quickly fortified by a few cups of piping hot tea, he sploshed his way back to his Mini, leaving me with both a new awareness of how much about badgers I didn't know and a sparkling resolve about watching in winter. Tomorrow night, for instance!

17

Badger woodland in winter

But it simply wouldn't stop raining. Not the gentle refreshing downpours of summer, but the slashing stair rods of a wetter than average January and early February. Sodden pasture. Dripping woods. Soaked undergrowth and fallen leaves. Enough to dampen the resolve of any winter badger-watcher.

Every weather forecast was demoralizing. It seemed it would never stop raining. I continued to tramp round my seven setts, plus others I also knew about beyond our village and on the marsh. Still it rained. A road into the village was flooded, prompting people nearby to protect their homes with sandbags. Ditches filled and overflowed, turning fields into lakes, driving sheep under farmyard cover.

Then, the third week in February, spring arrived for what proved to be a couple of glorious weeks. More and more snowdrops and crocuses; impatient daffodils in our own garden; start of the dawn chorus at the bedroom window. Magic.

Tonight, I said to my wife, I'm definitely going tonight!

Having tipped off the farmer who owned the wood – there's no trouble from him, the very opposite, but he likes to know who's about – I gave myself plenty of time to settle at my watching point. Arriving in daylight was important, not just for crossing the brook twice, but because I wanted to keep my feet off runs and as far as possible away from areas clearly favoured by the badgers.

There was another reason, too.

To understand fully, you need to experience a wood in winter at nightfall, alone. No, it's not the eeriness, though this might well keep you wide awake by quickening your imagination. Rather it's the activity beneath the calm, the thunder of tranquillity, the restlessness that buttresses stillness. Superficially, nothing is happening. Yet alone in this wood, enveloped by fading light, I was constantly reminded that even in the depth of winter such a place was anything but asleep.

My watching point was the giant oak favoured by Martin, ten strides or so from the entrance he'd described as central to the whole sett. I looked again and again at its trunk, finally accepting that to climb it was beyond me and, I like to think, anybody else outside the SAS. I checked the direction of the breeze; no need for a piece of cotton to monitor swirling, a dead leaf attached to what looked like a strand of spider's web functioned like a windsock, conveniently close to remain visible as the gloom thickened.

And thicken it did, slowly, caressingly; slowly enough for me to witness without my red-filter torch the first surprise of my vigil, caressingly enough for me to feel more protected than threatened. In truth I wasn't expecting anything to happen for the first couple of hours at least. Quite apart from my understanding that badgers in winter emerge unpredictably, later rather than earlier, Martin had mentioned a boar recently killed in a road accident at half-past six at night, a time, he'd said, when badgers weren't normally about. He'd also made the observation that this death could well have been a happy release, since the victim, apart from decayed teeth, had been seriously arthritic and showed signs of having been savagely bitten at the scut, doubtless by another boar.

I glanced at my watch. Five-twenty. Plenty of time before the badgers emerged, if they showed up at all. Might as well concentrate on my surroundings, pick out the noises paradoxically emphasizing the peace and quiet.

A movement no more than twenty strides away. A vixen slipping out of a den surrounded by badger entrances. She stretched, gazed around, strolling over to a mound of the badgers' digging and trotted out of sight.

Two or three minutes later her mate shot from nowhere in the direction of the other end of the wood, his urgency suggesting he was already hunting. He'd picked up a scent. Mine? I wondered. Once more I settled, listened.

Rooks were going crazy at the rookery deeper in the wood.

A cawing crow flew directly overhead, perhaps agitated by my presence.

Dogs barked spasmodically; guard dogs, I knew, easily triggered by the most innocent passerby.

Traffic sped by on the road connecting us to the next village and an industrial centre beyond. As headlights pierced the twilight, I couldn't help but smile as I wondered how the drivers would react if they could see me, a field from the road, waiting to see badgers in *our* village!

A terrible scream came from the other end of the wood. Twice. First kill of the night for the foxes? If so, it was all over in a moment.

A new noise dominated, one I'd heard often before. Badgers digging? At five-forty! I peered into the semi-darkness. Nothing. Switched on my torch. Still nothing. Yet the digging or whatever periodically continued, getting nearer. Nearer. And a pair of eyes shone in the beam. Just for a moment. A badger already?

I told myself not to be a fool. It was much too early, not

even really dark, nowhere near six-thirty. Calm down, I laughed at myself. Within a minute or so, no more, there it was again, the same noise, definitely coming in my direction. Again I switched on the red beam . . . and a badger stared into it, promptly decided to ignore it and continued its labours. It was rolling bundles of leaves into a huge ball under its chin and between the forelegs. Finally it shuffled backwards towards an entrance – not the central one I was watching. *She* passed me within no more than three strides, with the beam focused directly on her, and disappeared over the mound marking the entrance, too preoccupied wrestling with her obstinate load to care tuppence about me.

Bedding for her cubs? What else! But surely by now, cubbing imminent if not already accomplished, such an essential was long taken care of.

Before I'd time to ponder this conundrum, the sow repeated the exercise, again passing me almost within touching distance, contemptuous of my red light. And minutes later another sow, altogether bigger and stockier – still to cub? – did the same from another direction en route for a different entrance.

It was, I carefully noted, seven minutes to six.

After barely a break, a third badger, possibly the same larger sow, working frantically, provided a prolonged sighting as she gathered leaves and rolled them below, careless of me and my torch.

And then there *was* silence, teasing my mind, causing me mentally to flip over the pages of Ernest Neal's book. Why bedding now, so near cubbing if not past it? Didn't make sense, not immediately, not until the penny dropped.

Of course! The weather of the past six weeks. Constant rain, dripping wood, besodden undergrowth; mud making every outdoor venture an invitation to discomfort, doubt-less for badgers as well as humans. No wonder the taking of *dry* bedding below was delayed!

Obviously the past three or four days – premature spring – had worked the transformation; and badgers were at last able to find suitable bedding for their cubs.

Such reflections crashed to a halt at a sound not unlike *human* footsteps in autumn leaves. My heart palpitated. I peered. Nothing. Just the noise. Getting nearer. And into view came the outline of a man with a dog. Digger? Baiter? I couldn't be sure. In that brief moment the possibility seemed real, coupled, I have to confess, with the fear that if such was the case and I was discovered I was for the high jump. All the material I'd read, never dreaming it might one day apply to me, had warned that badger-diggers could be vicious with more than their four-footed prey. Better not to challenge directly, but keep out of sight, making careful note of incriminating evidence.

The man appeared to stare in my direction, apparently unsure. I crouched lower. His dog sniffed the breeze.

Couldn't be a badger-digger, I reassured myself, not here, not in our village. We didn't have any badgers. In any case, the nearest reported digging had been miles away. Even so, I couldn't forget Martin's warning that persecution of the badger appeared to be on the increase, not least in parts of Kent!

My heart continued to race, stimulated by further accounts I'd recently read of a woman watcher again being brutally attacked as she'd tried to frustrate diggers. If such people would beat up a woman, what hope for me?

At the same time I was also aware that a perfectly innocent passerby in a lonely wood at the dead of night might well be scared out of his life by my sudden appearance from behind a tree! What to do, when the last thing I wanted was the need to explain my presence at all, never mind at the very time I was hoping to welcome the badgers back?

Who was he? I wondered. Poacher? Villager taking a shortcut home? Actually a digger? As he receded I settled for villager. Had I known then what was soon to be revealed up the road from our village, I shouldn't have rested so easily.

Once more I heard footsteps in fallen leaves. Behind me. Slightly to my left. Coming nearer. I switched on the red beam.

The sow, also huge, stopped her labours, looked into the light, hesitated for a moment and was gone. In a flash. She was, I realized, in direct line to pick up my scent!

No use hanging about now. The entire sett would be alerted. But finding my way out of the wood, marvelling at my good fortune, I could hardly wait to watch again. The next time, I resolved, would somehow be from a perch high enough for my scent to be blown well above the most sensitive nostrils.

Reaching the fallen tree spanning the brook, I was about to step out when a badger appeared on the other side, also unmistakably intent on crossing. It stared hard if not defiantly into my red beam, for all the world as though protesting, not about the directly focused light providing me with a perfect view, but about the inconvenience of being kept waiting. Which of us was to go first?

For an endless ten seconds or so we stood facing each other, neither backing off. I was fearful any movement of mine might alarm the badger; the badger was perhaps unsure about approaching the light. The breeze was blowing my scent behind me, adding to the badger's puzzlement. It sniffed, lifted its snout, inhaled a bit more;

196

nothing. Meanwhile I waited. After you, Claude. No, after you . . . It really did strike me as being that kind of situation. For ages.

I feasted my eyes.

The badger tried to make up its mind.

Come on, I silently shouted.

Clear off, it seemed to answer.

I wanted to back off, but knew this was more likely to scare than oblige. So I stayed. Like the badger.

In the end, increasingly aware of an invisible, inexplicable barrier to its safe crossing, it decided discretion was the better part of vigour. It backed off rather than turned, and disappeared into woodland on the other side of the bubbling divide.

The next afternoon I returned to the sett of the galls to follow up the two paths that had appeared to peter out during the hurried search with Martin. Which just goes to show the importance of persistence. One path led me to what was clearly a feeding area, and then, out the other side, to two entrances both marked by recent digging. By the badgers! These in turn introduced me to more paths which led back to the bramble with galls, indicators of badger activity the whole way.

In celebratory mood, my dog at heel, I rejoined the disused track, rounded a bend, and froze!

A badger. Lying within two or three strides of an entrance, not far from the hole down which I'd seen the fox cub dive.

I looked. Hard and long. Trying to register the evidence of my own eyes. It was early afternoon!

Still the badger didn't move. Yet it looked alive; nothing suggested illness or injury.

Stealthily, my eyes on those front claws, I crept nearer.

Nearer. Not a flicker from the badger. Was it dead? A dead badger in the middle of a wood? What about the usual tomb underground or the grave above reputedly made by grieving badgers? My mind was racing. This didn't make sense, not to me. The badger itself looked perfect, not a mark anywhere, nothing to indicate it wasn't merely asleep. Yet common sense told me this couldn't be the case. The badger was either unconscious or dead.

Cautiously I turned the body over, no sign of rigor mortis. It was supple and, I discovered, still warm. I examined its eyes, jaws and teeth. As far as I could make out, the sow was a yearling, judging by size and dentition. I turned the corpse over and over, searching for clues, sick at heart, baffled, possessed by a mixture of awe and horror. The only signs of injury were a lacerated scut – possibly the result of a fight, but surely too superficial to cause death – and a tiny hole in the right temple.

Bullet? Pellet? Canine tooth mark from a fight? Even, as a friend of mine later suggested, evidence of a crossbow? I didn't know what to think.

The following weekend, accompanied by two grand-children and their father visiting from the city, I returned to the spot. As we almost reached it, the children, until now typically irrepressible, whispered and tiptoed. One had never seen a badger of any sort before. The other, my six-year-old veteran badger-watcher, now all of seven, stared at her first badger corpse. Their eyes flashed accusingly in my direction. Why didn't I do something? Bring the badger back to life?

Modestly I admitted that even grandads had their limitations . . . and queried whether – more realistically in the circumstances – it might be helpful to lift the body from near the entrance to the undergrowth and cover it with leaves?

I lifted.

The children did the covering.

Never had a badger received such reverence.

As we withdrew I mentioned badger funerals, and wondered whether on this occasion the badgers would bury their dead.

During the following weeks I returned repeatedly. The leaves slowly blew away, exposing more and more of the corpse. Inexplicably it appeared undisturbed even for carrion. And with no bluebottles and the like to pack its orifices to raise it from the dead, it steadily disintegrated, helped by legions of beetles and doubtless birds grateful for black and white nesting snugness.

Not a sign of a badger funeral!

After one such visit I decided to make a homeward-bound detour in search of a woodman I'd come to know and respect not only for his skill in traditional woodland crafts, but his whole philosophy of life. A gentle man, happy with his lot, as contented as it's possible to imagine a man to be. He was taught his skills by his dad, who was taught by his dad, and so on, a family heritage going back for generations.

Funny thing, I hadn't come across him for weeks, not sight nor sound; and when eventually I found his tarpaulin-covered mobile workplace it was wind-blown and nearly collapsed.

I was bothered. All the time I'd known him he'd virtually never missed a day's work, Monday to Friday, first light to the completion of his daily target, usually by mid-afternoon. Regular as clockwork. Normally alone in the woods for hours and days at a time, he was – I liked to think – always glad to see me; but no matter how animated our conversations, he rarely stopped working. That daily target worried him, until as usual he reached it. Then he went home to get a good night's rest in preparation for the next day's output!

I've met few men so satisfied with so little, grateful, as we say, for small mercies. Not that he thought of them as small. Wife, children, grandchildren, enough work as self-employed craftsman to pay his way, enough to buy annually a week's holiday in the sun, otherwise he didn't always bother about even bank holidays and the like. Happier in the woods, he used to laugh.

So the hanging tarpaulin looked ominous.

Life, it has to be said, sometimes plays dirty tricks, not infrequently against persons deserving of the extreme opposite! This woodman was, my enquiries revealed, a case in point.

For long enough I'd known of his secret dream, a sort of fantasy, to move from the industrial town in which he lived to a cottage in the country, a place reflecting the peace and quiet of his beloved woods. Understandably his wife wasn't keen. Brought up in the town, she felt more at home with close neighbours always ready for a chat, and with shops conveniently just round the corner.

But eventually, her health not so good, hoping that a complete change might bring improvement, she agreed. Perhaps the housing department could arrange a swap. After all, with so little work in the countryside these days, there must be lots of people on the look-out for a chance to move.

And so it proved. They were offered a house with a large garden, more than big enough for him to grow vegetables and lots of flowers – another secret hope he'd long accepted as being out of the question.

It all seemed too good to be true. Yet it *was* true, as the unloaded furniture van standing at the door proved. A perfect setting for him. A chance for his wife to convalesce. He could barely wait to start knocking the garden into shape.

The doctor told him the pains in his chest were angina, a warning he mustn't ignore. He explained that, being self-employed, he couldn't afford to rest. You must, advised the doctor.

The dilemma was resolved a few weeks later. He found he wasn't seeing so well, either his daily paper or the TV. The doctor diagnosed cataract in both eyes. You mustn't drive, he was told, not until after the cataracts matured and were removed. So he couldn't work. His wife, no transport but the rare country bus, was cut off from all her friends. The garden was running wild, in itself a major anxiety for a man haunted by untidiness and the frustration of not being able to do anything about it. And he worried about his job, money, losing his contract for work in the woods, his wife being stuck in the middle of nowhere, barely knowing a soul, his heart, his eyes, his family . . . Where would it all end?

One unsung man, inoffensive, asking so little of life, suddenly plunged into an abyss not remotely of his own making, an abyss offering no escape.

I was in the same area of the wood the other day; the tarpaulin, more of it dislodged from its collapsing wooden structure, flapped in the wind, like a lament or – as I chose to hope – to herald better days for the craftsman whose lonely workshop once echoed with the silence of content-ment as much as industry.

18
A digging mystery

The man I'd spotted in the wood at night with his dog
suddenly took on a possible new meaning. Shortly afterwards a police car bumped its way up the track to our front
door. Although this was unexpected, I wasn't altogether
surprised. Our village copper believes in community policing, meaning simply that he pops in, drops in, chats over a
cup of tea, shares the latest news, warns us, admonishes
us, generally puts us in the picture, all with the leisurely
air of a man who isn't wasting his time. Take it from me,
there wasn't much going on in our neck of the woods that
the arm of the law didn't know about; and what he didn't
know wasn't worth the bother.

He climbed from the car, adjusted his HF radio and
introduced me to a possible police force recruit, who
immediately underlined his humanity by asking for the
toilet. This accomplished, we sat down to drink tea. A
purely social occasion, I supposed, all part of our village
policeman's method of keeping law and order. Preventative
policing.

But I was wrong.

'Have you heard?' he asked.

I hadn't.

He filled in the details.

'Would you,' he wanted to know, 'like to see for
yourself?'

I should mention that our village copper is a keen ornithol-
ogist, has been for most of his near forty years. One

evening in my favourite wood, en route to what I hoped was a badger sett, I saw a face staring at me through the trees. My empty laughter hardly concealed my initial fright as the arm of the law identified himself, present to keep his eye on a pair of hobbies, rare visitors indeed in our part of the world.

That encounter indirectly illustrated not only his love of natural history, birds in particular, but the secret of his success in upholding the law. You see, he knows everybody, and everybody knows him, knows and therefore trusts him. Which explains why, following up a clue he gave me in the wood that night about another possible sett beyond the next village, I made headway. Otherwise, beyond doubt, the old lady living alone who reputedly owned the spinney containing the sett would have ignored me when I rang her doorbell.

She shuffled to a window, her eyes cold and suspicious.

'The badgers,' I said, 'in the spinney!'

The window, I noticed, was double-glazed and sturdy, built as much for security as excluding draughts; typical of the entire house, where everything was locked, a burglar alarm conspicuous on the wall. No way was this old lady going to open her door, safety chain or not.

I explained, shouting his name, our village policeman had sent me.

The transformation! She smiled broadly, relaxed, bade me welcome; and in no time I had permission to look to my heart's content.

'I'd be glad if you'd take a look,' the policeman said now; and arranged to pick me up on the following morning.

A police car coming to our cottage on two consecutive days, the first time for a fairly lengthy visit, the second promptly to take me away! Was it only my imagination that saw one or two curtains shiver as we passed? In truth, I myself, unaccustomed as I was to travelling in police cars, was sufficiently curious about what was to happen as I tried, as the saying goes, to help with enquiries, that I overlooked an immediate requirement of the law. A friendly voice put me wise.

'You'd better put your seat belt on,' it said. 'We might meet a policeman.'

We drove through our village, bypassed part of the next, turned down a winding lane and stopped outside what was once a farmhouse. The copper changed into his wellies, permanently in the boot for such occasions, rubbed my dog behind the ear and strolled across the road to meet a man clearly awaiting our arrival. A team of tree surgeons was working on devastation caused by the October hurricane, and – by the look of things – would be fully occupied for months to come. The aftermath of that one night still took a bit of believing.

We walked through a field, then a second, and into a spinney with sparse trees.

It happened here, said the man. And I looked at unmistakable evidence of badger-digging by other than badgers!

Walking his two or three acres, this relative newcomer from the city explained he noticed signs of recent digging and a hole filled in. Mystified, he went for a spade and started carefully to turn over the soil, somehow aware, for all his inexperience of living in the country, or perhaps suspicious because of it, that this was ominous. Two feet or so down he found what resembled offal, gathered it in a plastic bag, which he stuck in the deep freeze, and phoned the police.

What was it?

No doubt. For a start there were four badger foetuses, mixed up with the innards of a badger. No corpse. No pelt.

Just the innards and the foetuses. This was confirmed by a post mortem in which Martin and a friend of his, another expert, were involved.

So what had happened? The sow had reopened an outlying sett for cubbing. Someone, doubtless helped by at least one dog, had dug her out. Not only that, he (surely not a woman) had then spaded the sow to death, and with the same blunt spade, again confirmed at the post mortem, de-gutted her. Then he had buried the evidence and taken the body. It all took some believing!

Yes, but who? The village policeman said he had his suspicions, had in fact already spoken to the one he thought was concerned, who'd looked shifty and as guilty as hell. But how to prove it? So far, our arm of the law had put the fear of death into him, otherwise, unless more evidence was forthcoming . . .

So much I understood. But why the de-gutting? And the removal of the corpse?

To make the pelt a sort of prize exhibit? Hardly, unless the culprit wanted to attract attention to his unlawful activity.

To hang up alongside crows, weasels, magpies and other 'vermin' as deterrent to all reputed predators of pheasant eggs and chicks? Again, not unless the keeper concerned didn't care about the law protecting badgers, though – as our village copper pointed out – it was difficult in such circumstances to prove that the badger hadn't been found already dead from natural causes or a road accident.

Perhaps to sell to a taxidermist? Mounted specimens, lawfully acquired, are apparently in great demand.

All this apart, the de-gutting itself, never mind the viciousness and cruelty of how it was done, was a mystery. Even the so-called *responsible* digger would – you remember, it was claimed – either transfer the badger to a less populated area, kill it because it was diseased, or release it to provide more 'sport' for its only real predator on another day. I didn't believe a word of it, but at least it revealed a degree of conscience. This de-gutting was something else. What in the world could possess anyone to behave in such a fiendish manner?

The owner of the spinney and the policeman shared my bewilderment, though the policeman did make the point that nothing surprised him these days, even in our lovely, slumbering, law-abiding part of the country. Nothing. But he still seethed with anger.

The three of us wandered over the environs of the sett. A badger run led to woodland on the far side of a field, where pheasants were reared for shooting. I only wondered. Probably no connection at all. Indeed, in my admittedly limited experience, gamekeepers are no less responsible than the most committed conservationists. It's the occasional exception who causes the trouble, casting doubts on the lot.

We retired to the farmhouse to drink tea. The village copper rolled himself a fag, took a puff, sank a second cup, and turned up his HF radio. An emergency call to a suspected break-in six miles away. The police car sped off, leaving me to empty the pot and start my own six-mile journey. On shanks's pony. Actually, I needed that walk to calm down a bit and get my thoughts together before phoning Martin.

Why the de-gutting? I asked him. Wasn't this unusual, bizarre?

His answer, reflecting the opinion of the other expert also involved in the autopsy, added to my astonishment. True, it was only a speculation, Martin emphasized – nothing else was possible, given the circumstances – but he and his friend, having consulted at length, were agreed.

Badger hams!

'Sorry?' I said.

'Badger hams,' he repeated. 'An old country delicacy. Reputedly the hams are cooked in honey, and often smoked. We think the man who de-gutted the badger might have wanted its hams!'

'You can't be serious,' I said.

But he left me in no doubt that he was, deadly serious.

Further enquiries confirmed that this *was* an ancient country recipe, in the days when badgers, far from being protected, were thought fair game for all and sundry. Nevertheless, I still find it hard to believe that anybody would bludgeon a badger to death and rip out its innards with a spade – for its hams!

I have to confess, my heart was somewhat lifted as I legged those six miles home by remembrance of the slightest movement of a curtain here and there as the police car had bumped its way back to the road from our cul-de-sac dirt track. Talk about neighbourly concern! Not a nosy parker in sight, you understand. Genuine neighbourly interest of the sort that belongs inescapably to fishbowl living in a tiny community. What you might call natural curiosity, no more, no less.

So, sick at heart, I nevertheless chuckled as I thought of the speculation provoked by my being carted off by the village copper. Arrested? Taken in for questioning? For what? And such thoughts, I tell you, released waves of affection for our caring neighbours.

As communities go, our cul-de-sac takes a bit of beating; a happy band of unrelated brothers and sisters if ever there was one, mutually anxious to maintain at least good relations if not downright harmony.

Paradoxically, this brought to mind a spot of renewed

bother between two of our number about a garden fence; playful dog on one side, an assortment of exotic bantams and the like on the other. Nothing wrong with the dog, less still the exotic lovelies. It was simply that the dog, being a pedigree retriever, was mindful to consort with the lovelies. Not that she meant them any harm; the fun was in the chase, enlarged for her as they scattered squawking in all directions at once. And even when she actually caught one, again she meant it no harm; her jaws snapped with the gentleness of her breed.

Unfortunately, being essentially a family pet, accustomed to retrieving no more than an occasional boot or slipper, out of practice with the real business of her pedigree, she didn't know her own strength any more than how to curb her enthusiasm. Which posed problems for the lovelies.

The first time this happened, the wife of the infuriated owner on one side of the fence sloshed five corpses into the face of the dog's mistress on the other, merely to make a point. The dog wasn't welcome. So once more the fence was reinforced, a veritable Fort Knox, every possible means of penetration precluded.

Make no mistake, altercations in the countryside are caused by nothing more than doting owners outraged about the welfare of their animals, domestic pets or farm stock. On this occasion each of the main antagonists was left in no doubt about the feelings of the others involved, though – our secluded little community being what it is – harmony was quickly restored. Fairly quickly. Almost restored. The owner of the lovelies (and they *were* magnificent, hard to replace) continued without concealment to feel less than kindly disposed towards the unpractised retriever. As for *her* owners, they not only regularly checked the fence, but henceforth allowed the dog out of doors only under their personal supervision. Twice daily. Their vigilance was absolute.

We all sympathized with both parties, and hoped for a speedy return to our customary harmony.

To this end, the retriever's mistress settled into a routine whenever she left the house. First, check that the dog was indoors; then close the *two* doors separating the playful delinquent from temptation. No need ever to lock them, of course, not where we lived.

One morning, shortly after her departure for the village post office, someone knocked. The dog barked a greeting. More knocking. More barking. Strange, thought the caller, must be no one in!

And this posed a problem. He'd come a long way, was in a hurry, knew exactly what he wanted and where to find it. Furthermore, being a friend of the family, he didn't think anyone would mind if he saved himself the trouble of coming back; probably be laughed at if he didn't.

Within fifteen minutes the village post office patron returned.

The knock on the door sounded urgent. Impatient.

And she found herself looking into the face of a man with an armful of dead lovelies.

Oh, no, she groaned.

It took an eyewitness, another neighbour, to convince her. After all, she'd only been out for minutes, and the locked-in dog had still been there when she'd come back. But the neighbour, alerted by the hubbub, had seen the dog, with a lovely in its mouth, being chased by a man and his wife on the other side of the fence, with murder in their eyes. The dog dropped corpse number five in her wake, and – unable to return home, the innocent caller having carefully closed the doors before leaving – had shot into the watching neighbour's house and wisely stayed out of sight until granted a safe passage home.

The tally of lovelies so far? Fourteen.

Now you'd think, wouldn't you, no matter how tolerant and harmonious our little community, that blood of another order would flow? And you'd be almost right. Only almost.

The outraged owner of the lovelies was adamant.

The dog-owner's devotion to his pet was fiercely undiminished.

They talked. Negotiated; and in the end hit upon a compromise.

The dog must go. NOW.

So the dwindling number of survivors returned to their preening. The dog sought new sport, with a family of urbanites who'd always wanted a pedigree retriever. As for the main contestants, loving their animals as they do – and did – they're doing their commendable best to live and let live. It can't be easy.

As you would expect, most dogs hereabouts aspire to be nothing more than man's best friend. Theirs is not to reason why, despite their sometimes near human intelligence making spoken commands unnecessary. Whistle, nod or gesture, and they're away, a picture of eager and happy obedience compelling second and third glances of admiration.

Such a dog belonged to the joint owners of a craft shop on the borders of the next village. I imagine her background of farm work had a lot to do with it, but even this couldn't wholly acount for her comprehensive skill and understanding, typical of her breed, a sheepdog of mixed ancestry for generations! She seemed to walk to heel, always alert, as naturally as her owners strode ahead on the assumption she

210

would remain there until told otherwise. Then she was off like a rocket, no need for more than a whispered command.

The craft shop itself was very special. A fairyland. A centre of aromatic loveliness. An aesthetic experience. Behind the counter sat, almost invariably, the female half of the joint ownership. Their policy of never remotely pressing potential customers meant that everyone lingered to look, to feel, to smell, if not to buy. The male proprietor, a born non-seller if ever there was one, relieved his wife behind the counter only unavoidably, never with more than ardent reluctance.

'Shan't be long,' she promised one Monday morning, chosen because normally this was the least busy time of the week.

He dangled baskets and the like on hooks outside the shop, and settled with a book, hoping for a dearth of customers.

The doorbell clanged. He looked up, and caught his breath. The woman, accompanied by a boy and a girl, was stunningly beautiful, perhaps a model or an actress, and dripping wealth. She picked up this and that, wallowed in the herbal soaps and spiced fragrances, finally settled on a number of items – price was clearly no object or even consideration – and brought out her cheque book.

The man behind the counter reached for the calculator, tried three times with different results, fell apart, and nominated the middle figure. She started to write. He realized a serious error. Apologized. She tore up the cheque, and – not trying to hide her exasperation – started to write another.

As she signed her name he became massively aware of an appalling smell drifting its unstoppable way across the counter.

She looked up accusingly.

211

The offence gathered strength.

He wanted to explain. The dog. Under the counter, out of sight. But as he listened to himself silently rehearsing what to say, he knew she wouldn't believe him; probably despise him for blaming the poor creature unable to speak up for itself. He said nothing, frantically packed the carrier bag, handed back the bank card, and creased his face into a sickly smile.

She herded the children to the door, cast a look of contempt over her shoulder, and gulped fresh air as she stepped outside.

The dog whimpered in the middle of a dream.

'Everything all right!' beamed the returning half of the joint ownership.

Her face dropped.

She held her nose.

'The dog,' he explained.

'Oh, yes,' she said.

19

Badgers in the pigsty

The rather garbled information was tantalizing, prompting
a return to the Fort Knox I'd penetrated simply by mention-
ing our village policeman's name. The old lady was no less
suspicious until I shouted the same name through the
double glazing. Chains rattled. Keys were turned. And I
was advised, a finger pointing to the horizon, to get in
touch with a cottager living 'over there'.

I was making my way back to the road when I heard
voices of what, it transpired, was a radio play. The listener
looked up from her gardening, switched off the play (boring
anyway, she said), and wished me good afternoon. I
mentioned badgers.

'You want to talk to Mrs Dove,' she smiled. 'Lives in that
direction,' and she also pointed inconclusively. I heard
repeated the vague details of my enquiry; of Mrs Dove
rescuing four badger cubs after their mother had been
involved in a road accident.

Back home I consulted the phone directory, and dialled
the only possible number.

'Mrs Dove here,' a voice said. 'Badgers! No, not badgers
. . . I saw a great spotted woodpecker the other day . . .
think it was a great spotted woodpecker . . . might have
been a jay; hard to tell. But not badgers, not round here,'
she was emphatic. 'More's the pity! We're interested in
wildlife, conservation, that sort of thing. Badgers, you
say . . .'

I asked around the village. No one had heard of either
Mrs Dove or a badger involved in a car accident. The only

doves around here, I was assured, were my own. In the dovecot outside our front door.

And that, I imagine, would have been that, but for a woman living in an isolated cottage not all that far from Fort Knox. As I walked past it one early afternoon to check a sett after the October hurricane, she was in her garden and actually brought up the subject of the rescued cubs. This time, however, the name she gave me was Mrs Duff.

'But please,' she instructed me, 'don't bother her at the moment, she's busy nursing a sick friend.'

Two days later I attended a public lecture on badgers, in foreign parts seven or so miles away. Waiting for it to commence – the speaker (Martin), it was announced, was delayed in a traffic jam – I chatted with a man and his teenage son whose main interest in badgers was their wish to photograph them. They talked in technical jargon I didn't altogether understand, and were suitably astonished at my ignorance of several wildlife photographers whose names they mentioned with respect akin to awe.

It transpired they were from the same locality as Mrs Duff. Did they know her? No. The cubs? Again no.

Nearby a woman was chatting with one of the organizers of the meeting, a meeting, incidentally, aimed at starting a local badger group. They were turning over the pages of a photograph album, and she was providing a running commentary. I stepped round them to the display stall, interested most of all in an eight-to-ten-day-old badger cub killed a fortnight before by a dog and preserved in a display jar for educational purposes. Amazing. All the features were distinctive – black and white stripes, and, remarkable for their size at such an age, the front claws. No wonder they developed into such lethal weapons.

Somewhat sad, yet paradoxically grateful to be able to

linger over such a perfect specimen, I was brought back to earth as words wafted above the general hubbub . . . fascinating . . . marvellous . . . excellent . . . thank you, Mrs Duff. And I looked up to see the same official turning over more pages of her pictorial history of the badger cubs she rescued!

In her farmhouse a few days later I, too, turned over the pages while Mrs Duff, sometimes prompted by her younger daughter, described what she called one of the most satisfying experiences of her life. It all started, she said, in November, shortly after nine in the morning. Two men knocked on her door, the nearest house they could find. Up the road, they explained, was a badger . . . badly injured, unconscious . . . possibly dead. They weren't sure what to do!

Neither was Mrs Duff, apart from dropping everything, backing out her car and following them to the scene of the accident.

The badger was out cold right enough, barely alive, by the look of things, its head badly mangled and bleeding profusely, notably on the left side. The two men, already late for an appointment, but desperate to help, apologized profusely as they sped away, wishing Mrs Duff all the best with the badger.

She looked at it, still cogitating. If it was to be saved, the first step was to get it to a vet well known for his interest in badgers. Yes, but how? Suppose it was stunned or only dazed, sufficiently aware to lash out at the outstretched hand of the most kindly motivated rescuer?

This danger, fortunately, had crossed Mrs Duff's mind earlier, based upon her experience a couple of years before in saving a badger cub savaged by a terrier. Admittedly her main contribution then had been simply to deliver the victim to the vet, who himself had nurtured it to independence before returning it to the wild, but her frequent visits during this healing and rehabilitation period had demonstrated nothing more than the folly of arguing with a badger, even a cub.

So – forewarned – she arrived at the scene of this latest accident armed with the thickest pair of gloves she could find, normally used in the garden. And a sack.

Gingerly she lifted the unconscious animal, manoeuvred it not without difficulty into the hessian carrier, and drove home faster than maybe she should to phone the vet. Within minutes she was on her way to his surgery some six miles from her farmhouse.

Alas, by the time she tenderly emptied the sack on to the table in his consulting room, he was already miles away, responding to another urgent case. The badger, he'd briefed the surgery nurse, was to be given a painkiller and periodic whiffs of oxygen. Doubtless Mrs Duff would be happy to lend a hand. He'd return as quickly as possible.

The nurse inserted the needle.

Mrs Duff administered the oxygen.

And, nerves tingling, she had plenty of opportunity, waiting to give the next whiff, to take a long hard look at the sleeping form.

Surely, she thought. It must be. Her eyes continued to search for signs.

'This animal's pregnant,' she said, 'isn't it?'

The vet was noncommittal, about the badger's chances of survival at all, never mind the pregnancy. It was still deeply unconscious, its battered head, unmistakably the point of impact, indicating possible brain damage, the vet's greatest fear. He even consulted a neurologist friend of his, only to be told, hardly surprisingly, that all he could do at this

216

stage was keep the animal under close observation and hope for the best. Time alone would tell.

Mrs Duff visited the surgery daily, grateful when the badger became fully conscious, but concerned it showed few signs of life, and, ominously, was barely eating at all. She returned with a mixture of appetizers – including grapes and bananas – yet still the patient remained indifferent.

A week passed. The kindly vet explained there was nothing more he could do. The greatest need now was for constant observation and nursing, virtually twenty-four hours a day, something clearly beyond the resources of his busy practice.

Perhaps, he suggested, Mrs Duff would phone the RSPCA? They might be able to help.

She refused. Not that she had anything but admiration for the RSPCA; but stuck in her head were two considerations she couldn't escape. First, the badger was somehow her personal responsibility; and, second, if it was to have any chance at all it needed to be released as soon as possible at the scene of the accident, near where *she* lived. Better she care for the badger herself. The vet agreed.

So back to her farm she went, to prepare an old pigsty, long disused for its original purpose. The concrete floor she covered with sweet-smelling straw, knee-deep – enough, she calculated, for both warmth and a bit of tunnelling, if the badger felt so inclined. Then, armed once more with her thickest gloves, she returned to the surgery.

The still very sick animal, gently tipped from the sack to the straw, immediately disappeared below, as though trying to co-operate. But it wouldn't eat, no matter how tempting the menu:

Mince
Liver
Bananas
Bread and butter, with and without honey
Grapes
Eggs
A mixture of the lot

Nothing seemed to interest it. Nothing. Yet it was increasingly lively enough, apparently recovered or well on the way, inquisitive, venturesome, even playful each time Mrs Duff entered the sty. Nevertheless, no doubt absolutely famished, it wouldn't eat.

She consulted the book from the public library on badgers by Ernest Neal, and dug up worms, found slugs and snails, added dollops of honey to some of the other goodies on offer – all to no avail. The starving badger refused to be tempted. Soon it appeared, ironically, in serious danger of dying despite a full recovery from its injuries.

What to do? All she could think of was persistence; if at first or second or tenth you don't succeed . . . Yet again she prepared mince, peanuts, and liver cut into small pieces, then returned to the sty. She put the dish under the badger's nose. It tunnelled into the straw. She whispered endearments, pleaded, lifted the dish nearer, at times almost pushing it down the badger's throat. It remained indifferent. She separated a single piece of liver and reached towards the badger. It looked suspicious, sniffed, hesitated, and ate the morsel. And another. And another. Soon it was scoffing everything on offer, with the noisy gluttony of former occupants of the sty; stuffing herself silly.

And a further surprise was in store. Having eaten everything in sight, finally a colossal amount, the badger burped, an enormous burp whose volume and endless

duration caused Mrs Duff to struggle, not entirely success-
fully, to stifle her laughter in case she frightened the bloated
creature.

In truth, that burp still triumphantly re-echoes in her
head whenever she recalls that first feeding, for it marked
not only the end of the badger's fast, but the beginning of a
new and exciting relationship between the wild animal and
its rescuer.

Fortunately, in all the excitement, Mrs Duff never forgot
that the point of the whole exercise was the release of the
badger to its natural habitat. With this constantly in mind
she made her plans, thought out her step-by-step programme. First, an extension of the animal's freedom from
the inner sty to its outer confines open to the sky; then
periodic freedom in the entire farmyard; and finally total
freedom.

The first step went without a hitch, likewise the second,
until the badger proved less than co-operative by wanting
to extend the time in the farmyard. Mrs Duff, thick gloves
no longer necessary, didn't argue. She simply held her
dog's choke chain at the ready, the badger obligingly stuck
out its neck, and – with no further trouble – meekly trotted
back to the sty.

All too soon for Mrs Duff came the night of 13 February, a
date seared in her mind. Next day the badger must be
released. One final night in captivity, then back to the wild
where it belonged. Further delay was inexcusable. The
animal, fully recovered, was already dangerously human-
ized, happy if not actually preferring to be handled by Mrs
Duff, utterly trustful of her approach, too ready to entertain
and play with her, adding to the delights of their relationship.
No wonder Mrs Duff was compelled to acknowledge a
growing resistance within herself to the badger going!

Tomorrow, the 14th, was time to say farewell, before it was too late.

Locking the sty for the last time, she mentally rehearsed the simple method of release: final play session, sumptuous meal, and the door of the sty left wide open from early evening throughout the night. Definitely, she reprimanded herself for her half-heartedness, DEFINITELY tomorrow!

Shortly after dawn, feelings mixed, but happy for the badger, she returned with food to the sty. Despite the deep straw, the badger was clearly evident beneath it. But why all this noise – squeaks, squeals? Mrs Duff followed her ears. She parted the straw. Four badger cubs at the teat!

She bent closer, careful not to touch them or intrude, wondering what – if anything – she should do. She gazed at their pink skin with its faint suggestion of the distinctive black and white stripes, and was incredulous at their claws, seemingly disproportionate to the rest of their bodies. Their eyes were tightly closed. Each of the cubs hardly moved unless searching for a teat, made easily accessible as their mother lay on her side. A heap of new life.

Recalling that first glimpse, Mrs Duff relived her astonishment, the wonder of it all. Four badger cubs. In *her* pigsty. And now, conscience clear, there could be no question of the sow being released!

So began what this lifelong countrywoman, cultured, travelled, born with (some might say, though she would vehemently disagree) a silver spoon in her mouth, so began what she doesn't doubt was one of the greatest privileges of her entire life. There was so much to watch, to learn, by which to be charmed. But also an increasingly worrying snag. From the moment the cubs were born the sow again refused to eat, not a bite. Mrs Duff tried everything, from cutting up the liver into ever smaller pieces to ladling out the honey to sticking the dish under the badger's nose. Nothing helped. Yet strangely the badger's eyes seemed full of pleading, as though she was asking for assistance to provide nourishment for her greedy cubs.

Mrs Duff was flummoxed. There was nothing wrong, she knew, with the food on offer; before the cubs were born the sow was scoffing the lot on sight. Now she ignored it, though not, to add to the mystery, with indifference! Her eyes were full of hunger. Yet the overflowing dish remained untouched. It didn't make sense.

What, she puzzled, was she doing wrong? Or perhaps not doing right? She asked herself a hundred times, getting nowhere, worrying herself sick. And still the badger wouldn't eat. At this rate she'd lose her milk, and – despite her obvious devotion – starve her cubs to death.

The answer came fortuitously. Mrs Duff went into the sty with her customary dish of goodies. The badger didn't budge. Almost weeping with frustration, Mrs Duff once more separated a single piece of liver in the dish and leaned towards the badger. It devoured it with its eyes, but no more. Mrs Duff then placed the same piece of liver in the palm of her hand and reached forward. Unhesitatingly the badger took it. And another, lots of pieces, always and only from Mrs Duff's open palm. Why? Mrs Duff wonders whether perhaps the sow, looking upon her rescuer as the boar, was *waiting* in these early days of motherhood to be fed by her mate.

I simply pose the conundrum, knowing how sows can be fiercely protective of their newborn, keeping the boar at bay in case, as I mentioned earlier, he can't be trusted with the cubs. The fact remained, the sow in the pigsty wouldn't budge from the maternal nest, even though starving and with food so near to hand. Only when Mrs Duff actually fed her would she eat.

At the time, needless to say, Mrs Duff didn't care about explanations. Let the vet and Martin and other experts argue about *why* the badger wouldn't break its post-maternal fast; all she cared about was that food was being taken and transmuted into both strength for the mother and milk for the cubs. Soon the badger reverted to being her greedy self, scoffing everything on offer, handfed or not.

In all her enthusiasm, Mrs Duff resisted her own maternal wish to handle the cubs. They were, she kept reminding herself, *wild* creatures, born in her sty but destined soon to be released, to fend for themselves, to be exposed to hazards far removed from the security and hotel service of the pigsty.

If they were to have any hope of survival at all, they must be allowed to develop as naturally as possible, initially wholly dependent upon their mother, finally capable of taking care of themselves.

None the less it was simply impossible for some sort of relationship with Mrs Duff not to emerge, for the sow accepted her totally, proved by the freedom with which she allowed her near the cubs; and inevitably the cubs themselves, taking their cue from their mother, extended her welcome with playful ebullience. You might say, a good time was had by all, especially as the cubs – three sows and a boar – began to explore the outer sty, open to the heavens and with additional opportunities for wrestling, biting, pulling, scratching, shrieking in protest, chasing their own tails, or each other's – a popular early target – not to mention the four of them ganging up on their remarkably tolerant mother.

Round and round they would go, disappearing into the straw, emerging at lightning speed strides away and gleefully plunging on the next victim; the sort of games I myself had often watched by the hour and, like Mrs Duff, found better entertainment than the telly.

The one thing she now regrets – rather, one of two things – is that she didn't think to keep a diary. Her younger daughter did, the habit of a lifetime, but her job took her away from home for weeks at a time, making her written record of the badgers patchy, not to say tantalizing. Happily this doesn't apply to the weekly photographic record kept by her other daughter. Turning over the numerous pages, I too watched the cubs develop from a few hours old to the moment of their release; pictures galore in colour, illustrating rapid body growth, the beginnings of cubs exploring their surrounds at about six weeks, and the early co-ordination of limbs, smell, touch and hearing, resulting in soon quite remarkable energy and mischievousness.

I don't doubt that some of these wonderful photographs caused me to read into them my own experiences in watching cubs in our badgerless village; but having leisurely examined them, aided by Mrs Duff's comments, I well understood her claim of privilege.

Her other real regret? She neglected to switch on a tape recorder. At the time it never crossed her mind. She was too busy enjoying the badgers. Now, she could kick herself.

At about ten weeks the cubs became markedly less concerned about the physical presence or even nearness of their mother. While she slept or lounged in the straw, burrowing deeper for a bit of privacy and peace, they ventured, singly and together. Their circumstances were, of course, somewhat restricted, but this didn't curb their appetite for apparently knocking the living daylights out of each other, notably when squabbling over pieces of rabbit. Liver too was popular! How the two smallest survived some of the rough-and-tumble is a mystery, though without such high jinks they would have lacked enough toughness for the sty, never mind the fiercely testing world beyond it.

My eyes measured the sty, adequate in the circumstances, but undeniably restrictive as the cubs developed. What about dung pits? I enquired.

Ah, yes, the dung pits, she smiled; and proceeded to offer conclusive proof of her devotion. When they overflowed, meaning when the straw in always the same corner merited attention, she gathered it up for renewal. The badgers were very particular, she said; apart from that one corner. No trouble, she sounded matter-of-fact, just one of the pleasures of keeping badgers in a pigsty.

She calculated the cubs were weaned round about twelve weeks, though long before that they were showing more than a passing interest in their mother's solids, prompting the generous provider to increase the sow's rations. The mother was encouraged, often by handfeeding, to eat at least as much as she wanted. Her favourite by far were eggs fresh laid by Mrs Duff's own free-range hens. Not only did she guard them from the rampaging cubs by pushing them under her body, but she kept them till last, as though, it seemed to Mrs Duff, she looked upon them as dessert, *the* highlight of every meal.

(The mention of eggs made me wonder aloud what implications this represented for pheasant eggs, for instance. Perhaps a gamekeeper I know, badgers not exactly his first love, had a point after all! On the other hand, no one but a biased fool would dream of concluding anything from one sow's first preference from such a boring old menu as grapes, bananas and honey-coated bread, with or without butter.)

However, if this badger was addicted to eggs, her cubs, often the way with children, were crazy about Smarties.

They fought over them, made pigs of themselves with them, scrabbled in the straw for them as though not finding the most was at least a matter of life and death. In the end, wanting to introduce a bit of order and justice into the blood-letting, she served them on a table – a piece of wood dragged from the nearby spinney.

Peace if not fair shares for all remained as remote as ever. Yet *how* to prevent the boar cub from plundering almost the lot? From the start he was markedly more aggressive than the sow cubs, never allowing Mrs Duff too near. Whereas the others fussed around her, the mother to be handled, the sow cubs seeking similar treatment, he bristled with resentment, doubling his size by making his hairs stand on end, the usual ploy for badgers set on warfare.

She made no attempt to appease him. The last thing she wanted was badgers so trusting of humans they added to their vulnerability in the wild. The mother sow was something else. Having been rescued from death's door and nursed to robust normality, she *and* her cubs nourished by ample foodstuffs supplemented by worms and slugs, the mother accepted Mrs Duff unreservedly. Significantly, she one day gave every indication of wanting to leave the sty for good, with growing urgency. As though, according to Mrs Duff, she was trying to say, time to go.

This might have been her wish to mate, I suggested, as badgers – I was happy to explain! – come into season soon after giving birth, for four to six days at a time, but equally likely she was simply bored, responding to her own fundamental nature as a *wild* animal; perhaps a combination of both. Whatever, Mrs Duff needed no persuasion. As much as she hated the thought of losing the sow and her cubs, she knew and accepted that delay even by a single day was unjustified, a denial of her concern for the badgers' welfare.

That very night – 29 June – the pigsty door must be left open.

The final meal was delightfully riotous. There was lots of food, the badgers, unmindful of Mrs Duff's nearness, scoffing it all like pigs, and then engaging in their usual playful exercises, a veritable pantomime for their enchanted rescuer. She laughed out loud. She almost choked. Her eyes misted. She fought back the tears. This was *it*.

Dragging herself away, with half-hearted resolution she pushed the door wide open. Not looking back, she strode to the farmhouse. It was late; late enough for bed. But she didn't sleep, barely a wink. And well before first light she was back at the sty, desperately hoping the badgers were still there!

She found herself weeping, delighted they were where they belonged, sick at heart they were gone; weeping, despite her tough temperament and her lifelong involvement, as country child and farmer's wife, with animals of all sorts.

She ran to the woods behind the farmhouse, calling, making the noises she didn't doubt her badgers would recognize. She saw nothing. Heard nothing. The tears streamed.

Reliving that morning, for my benefit, she laughed at herself, at her sentimentality, the exact opposite of what a hardened countrywoman like herself was supposed to feel. It was ridiculous. But there was no hiding the emotional depth of that parting. The badgers were away. She was gratified beyond words. Yet bereft. The gap was hardly bearable.

All that day and well into the night she was on edge, listening, looking towards the pigsty, hoping they might return, not permanently, just for a brief visit to reassure her all was well in what she knew were crucial hours of adjustment to their natural habitat.

No news is good news, she kept telling herself; and laughed through her tears at the utter stupidity of being so affected by the fulfilment of what she had always wanted and planned. Deep within herself she celebrated, whooped like a child, told herself she was happy for the badgers. And she was, she was.

The fact remained, life without them could never be quite the same again, enriched but strangely empty. The pigsty, every time she passed it, was full of their absence.

Every night, after another day on the farm she and her late husband had worked for many years, Mrs Duff returned to the spinney and neighbouring woodland, hoping for renewed contact with her badgers, a contact in the *wild*. She knew from Ernest Neal's book that this was possible. He'd told of a cub brought up in captivity and eventually allowed free access to the countryside. At first it returned each morning, a little later about once a fortnight, finally not at all. But months afterwards, following complaints about a badger making a nuisance of itself in a garden, it was identified. The woman who'd brought it up watched it go into the garden and then the garage. Shut in, the animal became aggressive. Yet when she entered with her dog and called out in reassurance, the badger, appearing to recognize her voice, lost its anxiety; 'dog and badger sniffed each other amicably'.

So Mrs Duff, too, kept hoping as she called out at the spinney in the language peculiar to herself and her badgers. No response.

As days passed into weeks she became reconciled to never seeing *her* badgers again. Indeed, the pain eased, giving way to profound satisfaction at every remembrance of the entire episode, including their departure. Leaving the farmhouse one morning, she cast her customary glance at the pigsty. And gawped.

One of her cubs.

Virtually knocking on the pigsty door, not – needless to say – for permanent admittance, but FOOD. At least, it needed no encouragement to take full advantage of Mrs Duff's typical generosity. It lingered for a while, scratching itself here and there; then nonchalantly wandered off this time (as it proved) never to return – never, that is, unless this was the same cub involved in a fatal road accident months later. Mrs Duff couldn't be sure, though she doesn't doubt the victim *was* one of her cubs.

As night follows day, she is now known among her friends and the elect villagers let into the secret of the pigsty badgers as 'the badger woman', the person to whom to turn in all things to do with badger welfare. The latest road casualty brought to her doorstep was a boar found by a man and his wife out for a stroll. Whether injured in an accident or a fight with another badger wasn't clear, but in any case a week proved long enough to permit his release, a week during which, need I mention, he emphatically showed not the slightest inclination to be fed by hand or for an intimate relationship! Merely ate everything in sight, and did a bunk at the first opportunity.

Another success story.

20

Villagers, badgers, and the Channel Tunnel

I wish I could say the same about badgers in relation to the Channel Tunnel. It isn't, of course, merely the actual tunnelling, though in some areas this is concern enough, but the consequent upheaval on a much wider front. Reaching, would you believe, to the very doorstep of our village!

I stumbled across the threat – for badgers and wildlife generally, never mind humans – through a villager friend of mine putting her cottage on the market. The estate agent not only mentioned an astronomical price . . . is the world going mad? – but urged upon her the importance of selling NOW, before the ramifications of the Channel Tunnel reached us. Hadn't she heard?

No, she hadn't.

Well, he said . . . and the details took a bit of believing. Anonymous developers, looking at a map of the South-East, had simply pin-pointed the biggest patch of green nearest the desired area and planned to build thousands upon thousands of houses; they would swamp the village next to ours and the one beyond that, joining both to an industrial town miles away.

She found it hard to take seriously. What about planning permission? The green belt? Surely the authorities wouldn't agree. Her husband was reassuring. The estate agent, he smiled, would say that, wouldn't he? He wanted the business. But her sister wasn't so easily placated. She knew that the village next to ours was already organizing a protest meeting and otherwise planning to storm the forts of bureaucratic darkness. Destroy *their* village? Over their dead bodies. Nevertheless, pessimism was gaining ground. Already some villagers were hoping against hype, fearful of a takeover by big business, not to mention the estate agent.

Sell NOW, he kept repeating. Prices are bound to tumble. In fact, he was expansive, the village nearest the green belt chosen for development was in panic; prices were beginning to fall.

I confess I took all this with a giant pinch of salt. The whole idea was madness. Thousands of new dwellings bang in the middle of a *protected* area of outstanding natural beauty! The proposal was certain to be opposed by the parish council, the borough council and the county council, never mind every right-thinking public servant in the higher regions of government. Surely.

But then I met a farmer friend of mine as I tramped across one of his fields, en route for the wood containing my first-love badger sett – the one near a pile of rubble that was once a farm labourer's cottage. In five minutes he compelled me to see that the outcome was by no means certain.

First, he confirmed that developers had pin-pointed the area they wanted, the village next but one to us. Second, that things had quietly moved on apace since then. True, planning permission had not yet even been sought, through official channels. But there were other ways, essential preliminaries, what some people might call a frontal assault through the back door.

Farmers in the neighbourhood had been offered a business package: a thousand pounds an acre *now*, guaranteeing nothing more than a five-year option to buy the land outright – this outright price to be determined by the market value for farmland at the time of the purchase; the final deal to be contingent upon planning permission being granted. Ah!

Even so, any farmer, it seemed to me, would be a fool to sell. Building land was infinitely more expensive than farmland, worth a fortune. We already knew of one farmer who'd cashed in by selling a strip of his land to a consortium granted planning permission to extend an adjacent development. For any farmer with a mind to sell, wouldn't it be worth while to wait?

My farmer friend nodded. Smiled. 'It's a gamble, whichever way you look at it,' he said. 'The developers could lose their initial thousand pounds an acre if they failed to get planning permission, leaving the farmer with the money and his land. On the other hand, the farmer could lose the admittedly colossal difference between the price of farmland and building land. Yet again, both could gain! Suppose,' he went on, 'a farmer was nearing the end of his working life, with no family to inherit his, say, one-hundred-acre farm. He settles for a hundred thousand now, with the prospect of a similar payment within five years. After his lifetime of scrimping and saving, well . . .' his voice tailed away, leaving me to draw my own conclusion.

No doubt about the force of the argument, of course. The money would keep him in luxury, undreamed of luxury, for the rest of his life, his only problem how to spend, and spend, leaving nothing in the bank when he died! Any (no matter how inflated) price for building land wouldn't make a scrap of difference, not in ways that could essentially change his situation. Better for him to sell and be sure, especially if he knew running the farm was already becoming too much for him. In any case, if he put the farm on the market, he wouldn't do any better than the developers' offer; and that *immediate* down payment, no hassle, no need to leave the farm straightaway, would solve a few problems! And he might get a hundred thousand for nothing!

'Surely,' I reasoned, 'the developers couldn't afford to chance losing so much money, not when they must realize planning permission is almost certain to be refused?'

'Money's no object.' He laughed at my naïvety. 'They know right enough they'll be turned down by the parish council and the borough council and the county council, but this won't stop 'em appealing to the Department of the Environment; and with their sort of money to hire the best legal brains in the country, they'll find a loophole somewhere to get their plans accepted, sooner or later. I reckon,' he sounded philosophical, resigned, 'it's only a question of time.'

'And what about you?' I asked. 'Are *you* tempted?'

'Not bloody likely,' he said. 'It's different with me; my son shares my love for the farm.'

I wandered over another stile, and another, across a field of winter corn, and into the wood, my mind racing, my eyes seeing nothing. Was it conceivable? Our bit of England's green and pleasant land sacrificed to the developers? After-all, the Channel Tunnel *was* being built. People had to live somewhere. Nothing must stand in the way of progress. Profit.

At the sett I sat on a tree felled by the hurricane, my eyes darting from one entrance to another, gratified at all the signs of badger activity. What a place. Miles from anywhere, woodland tucked away and barely disturbed by human intruders like me. Ideal for badgers.

Sitting there, I remembered other setts I knew, some miles from our village, with a great variety of habitats reflecting the badger's remarkable adaptability to change beyond its control. The overspill of industrial centres and gobbling up of villages was making the urban badger increasingly numerous.

Where, though, would it all end? The question emphatically was no longer merely a conservationist talking point; it was applicable to unfortunates threatened in green belt garrisons elsewhere, miles from here. For if the developers could carve up the Garden of England, nowhere and no one was safe, humans no less than badgers.

With such sober forebodings I made my way back to the cottage. The phone rang. My wife. It was necessary, after all, she confirmed, for us to move again for a few weeks, possibly longer. The treadmill of earning a living.

'What about the badgers?' I asked.

'There'll be plenty more where we're going.' She sounded confident, even fairly sure, adding, 'Jenny and her family [who share my secrets and enthusiasm about the setts] will be only too pleased to keep their eye on them till we get back.'

And she could, of course, be right, about the badgers – where we've arrived, I mean. So far, all I can be sure about are the compensations of our no less isolated situation:

hares sitting on their haunches like small kangaroos – I'm amazed at their sheer size – or loping across the fields within view of our windows;

Canada geese honking as they fly over;

twenty ewes or so, *each* with triplets, the latter skipping, springing straight up on all fours, gambolling to their hearts' content, an irrepressible celebration of new life;

and now, that lot transferred to richer pasture to maintain bulging udders firing on at least three teats apiece, we have another twenty or so still waiting to lamb, with half a dozen already having obliged, one before our very eyes.

Inevitably in such an idyll, other elements are less pleasing, like the lamb that died two or three days after being born. We spotted it early one morning, its innards ripped out by a pneumatic drill camouflaged as a crow's beak, the marauder still bloating itself, spasmodically cawing satisfaction. What a mess!

Not that we blamed the black butcher. For being its natural self? This aside, we were almost immediately too busy trying to come to terms with something less straightforward. Had I seen the dead sheep? My wife shouted from the landing upstairs. At the gate not far from our cottage?

I looked. My eyes searched.

'At the *gate*.' She sounded somewhat incredulous. On the side nearest us.'

Still I saw nothing.

She descended like a dropped stone, and pointed.

'There!' she said.

'Where?' I asked.

'THERE!' She almost fell through the window.

I nipped outside, urgently, aware that time was of the essence. You see – though doubtless you know – sheep sometimes get down and can't get up; they wave their legs to futility like distress signals but haven't the sense to move their arses a little to one side for better grip. And the corpses aren't a pretty sight, judging by the couple I'd seen, faces rubbed raw in the struggle, eyes pecked out by the ubiquitous crows. In this case, there might still be time.

The only object near the gate was an old plastic bucket, admittedly sizeable, but nothing like a sheep.

'Is *that* what it is!' She seemed less than convinced. And we nearly choked laughing at the remembrance of the last such occasion.

'Look at that flock of sheep by the lake,' she had nodded.

'They're swans,' I'd said.

'Surely sheep,' she'd said.

'Swans,' I'd insisted.

So we had settled for a flock of white sheep with long thin necks and yellow beaks, a rather rare woolly breed known as Bewick's.

These misidentifications only occur, I hasten to add, when she takes off the glasses with which, according to family legend, she was born. With them on, she sees as well as anybody in the dark. Off, distant shapes play dirty tricks on her.

Anyhow, plastic sheep at the gate or not, we continue to enjoy our first few weeks here. BUT AS YET NO BADGERS.

Shortly after we arrived I asked a farm worker if she knew of any setts. I asked her because reputedly her lifelong knowledge of the entire neighbourhood was absolute.

'Badgers!' Her eyes filled with sadness. 'No, not round here.' She thought a bit more. 'The nearest badgers are at Dead Man's Wood,' she said; and proceeded to prove her knowledge of the district by giving me detailed instructions of how to get there, adding, *'We don't have any badgers in our village!'*

Now, where had I heard that before?

I think I'll keep looking . . .